ASIAN POLITICAL, ECONOMIC AND SECURITY ISSUES

USA - UNITED STATES OF ASIA: AN ASIAN UNION INITIATIVE

ASIAN POLITICAL, ECONOMIC AND SECURITY ISSUES

Additional books in this series can be found on Nova's website at:

https://www.novapublishers.com/catalog/index.php?cPath=23_29&series
p=Asian+Political%2C+Economic+and+Security+Issues

Additional e-books in this series can be found on Nova's website at:

https://www.novapublishers.com/catalog/index.php?cPath=23_29&series
pe=Asian+Political%2C+Economic+and+Security+Issues

ASIAN POLITICAL, ECONOMIC AND SECURITY ISSUES

USA - UNITED STATES OF ASIA: AN ASIAN UNION INITIATIVE

GUANG WU

Nova Science Publishers, Inc.
New York

Copyright © 2010 by Nova Science Publishers, Inc.

For permission to use material from this book please contact us:
Telephone 631-231-7269; Fax 631-231-8175
Web Site: http://www.novapublishers.com

NOTICE TO THE READER

LIBRARY OF CONGRESS CATALOGING-IN-PUBLICATION DATA

Wu, Guang.
USA : United States of Asia / Guang Wu.
p. cm.
Includes bibliographical references and index.
ISBN 978-1-60876-180-7 (hardcover)
1. Asia--Politics and government--21st century. 2. Asia--Social conditions--21st century. 3. Asia--Economic conditons--21st century. I. Title.
DS35.2.W817 2009
950.4'3--dc22
2009037457

Published by Nova Science Publishers, Inc. ✛ *New York*

Dedicated to my Beloved Parents Qinghe Wu and Heqing Zhou

If you want to go quickly, go alone. If you want to go farther, go together.
African Proverb

CONTENTS

PREFACE

After the initial reform in China by Chinese leader, Dong Xiaoping, the Chinese people had the opportunity to go abroad. However, this was not possible for the ordinary Chinese person who had no particular reason to travel abroad at that time. Thus, the Chinese people, who had been able to visit foreign countries, often wrote and told of their impressions and stories about other foreign countries; especially about the United States of America in various types of media.

During the last century in the 80s, a Chinese professor after visiting the United States of America told a newspaper reporter: 'China should divide her territory into 50 provinces because the United States of America has divided her territory into 50 states' without giving any further reasons. At that time, China had twenty-nine provinces and central-government-controlled cities. In another story concerning the United States of America, an author was deeply moved to write that the people who live in the United States of America as, 'living in paradise.' Facts about travel were that, the people who had a American passport could travel anywhere they like; but the people, who had a Chinese passport, could go nowhere. And those people that use the American dollar could buy anything they like; but the people, that use Chinese currency were actually forbidden to use it beyond Chinese border and could not buy anything.

These two stories in a way became a joke to us in China; if we, the Chinese, could rename China as the United States of Asia and divide China as 50 provinces; and then if we issue Chinese passports the same way as a passport from the United States of America. The only difference would be to let Asia replace America. However, this clever difference must be done as invisible as possible in order that we, the Chinese, could travel anywhere we dream! Yay! Ha! Ha!! Ha!!!

This fantasy dream could continue with reference to the American dollar, which is called either Mei Jin (American gold) or Mei Yuan (American dollar) in Chinese language. However, Yuan is a basic unit of Chinese currency, thus this fantasy would allow the Chinese to issue the Chinese currency as the dollar of United States of Asia, similar to the dollar of United States of America; only difference again would be to let Asia replace America. Once again, this clever difference had to be done as invisible as possible in order that we, the Chinese, could not only travel anywhere we like but also could now buy anything we want! Yay! Ha! Ha!! Ha!!!

This fantasy could be a dream for the Chinese people who hope to go to the United States of America. This could be the dream for the Chinese people who want to go abroad, and this fantasy dream for the creation of the United States of Asia could be a promising concept. Actually and, realistically, we know that the United States of Asia, cannot be the name for any Asian country.

As the years passed, this fantasy dream of mine would take this simple concept in another direction; that the Asian people could have the possibility to create an Asian Union, and is the topic of this small book.

In our previous books [1, 2], a request was made for no English editing, however, the Publisher kindly edited the English in this book. Therefore, my thanks go to the anonymous copy editor for her/his beautiful, clear and concise wording.

The author also wishes to thank Mr. Tianyu Wu at University of Udine, Udine, Italy for discussion on the book title.

Guang Wu
June 5, 2009, China

Chapter 1

RESHAPING OF ASIA

Asia, you are the place that had once given birth to three great religions, Christianity, Muslim, and Buddhism. Asia, you are the place that had once cradled three ancient civilizations in parallel, Chinese, Mesopotamia, and Indian.

Asia, you have since undergone a most shameful and humiliating history; colonized by various world powers, you have lost your identity in many ways over the years.

Asia today is the place with three economic giants, Japan, China, and India. It has rich oil resources in Saudi Arabia, Iran, and Iraqi. There are world-class city centers like Tokyo, Singapore, Hong Kong, Shanghai, Dubai, and so many others.

Asia, old in its history had the tendency to be slow because of its rich civilizations, and diverse cultures and their variety of traditions that not only produced huge inertia but still has the ability to attract people from around the world.

Asia, you are still vital and active because there are more eager young women and men with hope for a bright future living in Asia than in anywhere in the world.

People often refer to the 21st century as the Asian century [3]. However, how can the Asian people make this dream or claim to be realized now or in the next generation? Clearly, and perhaps realistically, a single more advanced Asian country will not make it an Asian century, as in Aesop's fables [4]: "One swallow does not make summer."

Hence, in order to make the 21st century an Asian century; Asian people need to enhance from a country level to a regional level, and then, as the next step, from a regional level to a world level. We need to reshape Asia, in order that Asia could once again make her great contributions to human civilization; by her cultures, religions, and economy, to world peace and prosperity as was done by our Asian ancestors.

For this brilliant future, Asian people need to consider how to approach their future rather than spend energy and time in trying to solve a long history of problems inherited from past generations. This is evident because a single year, or another generation, or the next century is not enough to solve the problems accumulated over years for that matter past centuries. Although it is important to recognize these old problems it could take unaccountable and unimaginable years to solve, and Asia would stay trapped in the past and lose the opportunity for a better future. In this brilliant future, some of these old problems would fade as we advance toward a better future, one major example is poverty.

Nevertheless, a history as long as Asian history, there are indeed many, even too many obstacles in each Asian country to keep our eyes from searching out ways to overcome these pretty old obstacles rather than concentrate on the future of Asia.

Honestly and quite frankly, there are indeed many problems within Asia; although they are consistently addressed at a national or regional level their solutions can only be found at an Asian level.

In fact, Asia as whole has many problems that need to be addressed at an Asian level. There is a need to create a platform to address the issues related to the entire region of Asia.

Up until now, not much attention was given to consider the serious possibility for the creation of an Asian Union as made evident in North America and Europe [5].

In this growing globalized world with its economy, Asia must Asialize our Asian countries first. Only then, would Asian countries have the real opportunity for global profit. This argument stands out because currently the main stream of Asian economy is orientated toward non-Asia countries.

Let us now focus on the problems inside Asia, and if there are any solutions to these problems.

1.1. PROBLEMS

To list all the problems within each Asian country would be an impossible job. It is not only because each country has too many problems to solve, but these problems exist at various levels from national level to individual level. However, it is reasonable to consider that even if we could solve all the local problems, new problems would arise. Even though every day the possibility that new problems could simultaneously arise the likelihood would be that some of the old problems could also be solved.

How can our generation of Asian people have sufficient time to solve all the past-generation problems and sort out the complicated ties between each problem? Again, this is an impossible demand for any great leader within their respective country. To be realistic and practical is to solve the problem at an Asian level and to push Asia to move forward because: (i) the regional problems at an Asian level would be arguably more important, (ii) the solution of problems at an Asian level would minimize the severity of problems at their domestic level, and (iii) most local problems might not be related to the 21st century which suggests that these old problems could be around forever.

1.1.1. Uniform Voice

The first problem for Asian countries is that the Asian people do not have a uniform voice that represents the interests of Asian people on an international stage. Also, it seems that there is no 'one' Asian country that can speak on the behalf of the other Asian countries on a international stage. A more pitiful, and perhaps sorrowful fact is that many Asian countries cannot even represent themselves on the world stage. Thus, how could there be a possibility to expect to see these Asian countries speak on the behalf of all Asian people. By clear contrast, we have witnessed the uniform voice from European Union, from NATO, from North America, from Africa, from South America, and Australasia. More sad and painful to witness is that some Asian countries seem to speak on the behalf of non-Asian countries to address problems generated within Asia and serve themselves as representatives for non-Asian countries. This could be the first rationale to reshape Asia.

Frankly, it would be hard to expect any uniform voice to represent these Asian countries on international politics, because each of these Asian countries have completely different views on the world. However, it is with sincere hope that Asian countries could address some common topics in a uniform voice. For example, Asian countries could address economic issues as a uniform voice on the behalf of Asian people; even if these Asian countries have different economic models and mechanisms. This would be possible since the economic model in most Asian countries is designed for countries outside Asia. Another universal issue that should be of interest to all Asian countries is an environmental concern, which must be solved in stages: first, at regional level, then at Asian level, and finally at global level.

This could generate a formal consensus among Asian countries on common economic issues as seen by the role that OPEC plays. This means that Asia could possibly have several consensus issues based on the same economic concern to address their similar problems at an Asian level. This could also open up the possibilities to have a common consensus among Asian countries on the environment.

Another big problem is the current UN cannot efficiently and effectively represent the interests of Asia, whose population accounts for a large portion of the world population and its industrial output accounts for a significant portion of the world's industrial output. However, it is only China that serves as a permanent member in the UN Security Council. This would suggest that many proposals on Asia are not discussed in great detail or with consideration for the view of many Asian countries whose interests and concerns are not clearly represented. Of course, many Asian countries could cast their votes based on their perspective concerns.

The direct result from the current UN structure suggests that the UN could pass any resolution without the approval from Asian people. The only consequence is that these UN resolutions cannot be efficiently and effectively implemented. A short-term solution to this problem should be a proposal for a regional UN in Asia to work in cooperation with any UN resolution at an Asian level. For this, there is a need to reshape Asia.

Basically, a uniform voice is needed to represent the interests of Asian people for the prosperity and peace in Asia and around the world.

1.1.2. Economic Slowdown

The second problem concerning the Asian people is how they can successfully and ecomonically defend against any possible worldwide economic slowdown, especially, when this worldwide economic slowdown often originates from outside of Asia. For example, the current worldwide economic slowdown originated in the US. The reality is perhaps a sad fact; each worldwide economic slowdown hits Asian countries badly, since the Asian economy is composed of many export-oriented industries and oil-export countries. Clearly, most Asian countries define non-Asian countries as their major markets. Thus, the export-oriented Asian countries suffer dearly during each wave of worldwide economic slowdown.

The influence of worldwide economic slowdown on Asia is not limited to one or two Asian countries, such as Japan, South Korea or China, but the influence generally ranges from East Asia to West Asia. By massive layout in export industries, a series of measures should be taken into considersation to find a way out for export industries. The solution to this problem could be found on an Asian level, since no single country has the ability to defend itself against a wave of worldwide economic slowdown.

The Asian people could make our industry not only be more competitive, but also be more Asian-oriented similar to the European Union; where most trades are conducted between European countries. Actually the huge population size in Asian countries would provide the biggest markets in the world for Asian industry, service, tourism and so on. However the problem that the Asian people have is that there is often no money available to buy and enjoy their own products and services. The crucial topic then is how to make Asian people have more money.

Still, the recent worldwide economic slowdown suggests an over all need for a more responsible globalization rather than just simply a globalization. In order to avoid a disaster in the world economy it is important to consider which kind of a globalization is essential. One that benefits only a dozen countries at the expense of other countries is one probable scenerio. Another scenario that is highly likely would be the globalization designed that aims to only benefit a small number of countries and create an imbalance rather than balance in global economy.

In fact, it seems that all the international organizations appear powerless and hopeless to prevent an economic slowdown or disaster. Thus the very question is: who will hold the responsibility for a fair globalization that would lead to the prosperity of all nationals in the world?

How can the Asian people face the possible economic slowdown originated from the rest of the world? How can the Asian people be immune to a world recession? These two questions should be the topic of focus for each Asian country to think about as an Asian concern.

1.1.3. Unbalanced Development

Asia perhaps has the most unbalanced ecomonic development in the world. In Asia, part of it has a very advanced economy as found in Japan, South Korea, Hong Kong, and Singapore. Unfortunately, the other extreme would be the undeveloped economy of Burma and Afghanistan.

In Asia, there are some countries that are heavily dependent on agriculture, other countries are heavily dependent on natural resources; then there are also countries which are heavily dependent on its financial sector or countries heavily dependent on export, etc.

Another important aspect within Asia is there are countries whose population decrease yearly, while there are other countries whose population can increase without limit. There are places in Asia where the population density is unbearably high, and there are other places where the population density is very low.

All these economic and population imbalances can provide Asian countries with great developmental opportunities. However, the general concern by Asian countries to these unbalanced developments is not, it seems, a particular interest to help address poverty in the underdeveloped Asian countries. Unfortunately, one piece of rationale is the market that leads the economic surge of immigrants, drug traffic, human traffic, prostitutions, etc.

If the Asian countries could somehow focus on addressing the unbalanced development within Asia, perhaps by discovering ways to create more employment; this could minimize the pains introduced from outside Asia. Actually it is because of this existing unbalance in economic development that provides the opportunity for investment; poor areas allow for cheap labor and access to cheap raw materials. In fact, all economic investments follow this line of thought in human history but, why do Asian people not want to follow this line?

Actually both the US and European markets are very crowded with highly competitive companies from around the world, and these profits have progressively narrowed. Why has Asian people not looked for the markets within Asia?

1.1.4. Endless Conflicts

There are few other places in the world like Asia, where endless conflicts make-up its history and where endless conflicts are hard to number. These endless conflicts and uncountable hotspots make Asian leaders and their people pay more attention to these conflicts and hotspots; so much so there is less energy and time spent on economic development within their Asian countries. Actually, there are a multitude of conflicts found in Asia; some sorry examples are due to differences in ideology, religions, ethnic groups, and clearly economic interests.

Tragically, there are hotspots with the potential for nuclear conflicts currently located in Asia, where the nuclear programs in North Korea and Iran impose the danger of war on a continental level. Still to consider is that these active wars and conflicts are mainly located in Asia, for instance, the war in Afghanistan and endless conflict between Palestine and Israel consume the life and energy of Asian people. Asian people can easily see the disadvantages of war and its endless conflicts. It is better instead to promote the need for economic development. We, as an Asian people, would rather not see these hotspots become the second Balkan and drag Asia further toward war either on a continental level or a world level. Asian people do not want to see Asia polluted by nuclear disasters led by nuclear war or by the attack on a nuclear facility in Asia.

Why is it so hard for the human race to live happily and peacefully? Where can this fantasy dream be considered? As a possibility, under the frame of United States of America and even under the frame of European Union, hold promising examples for the Asian people to live peacefully and happily in this great continent of Asia.

All religions teach us to live peacefully. Why religious conflict continues in Asia for so long, in so many places, to claim so many lives of innocent people is questionable.

In general, Asian people can be viewed as a more peaceful and perhaps weaker people. There is little history that documents aggressive colonization of other nationals. Actually, there is more evidence of being colonized by other nationals; the exception of course is the historical periods when the conquering Persian and Mongolia Empires had gone out of their Asian territory. Why cannot a peaceful-natured Asian people live peacefully together?

1.1.5. Death of Old Mechanisms

During this worldwide recession, one might naturally ask questions: (i) Is this recession the failure of globalization? (ii) Is this recession the death of WTO? (iii) Is this recession the death of economic model prescribed by super clever people who live outside Asia?

Of course, it could be too early yet to claim or even sentence the death of the old economic mechanisms. However, a strong remedy is certainly needed to restore the confidence of the old mechanisms and their reputation. Only then, could it function to service for a better future and allow under-developed countries to benefit.

Unilaterally, the under-developed countries or less-developed countries, even the developed countries need to search for the new ideas for future economic development.

The Asian countries need to seriously consider different ways for future development. This enormous task needs all Asian people to think about a remedy for our future.

1.1.6. Other Issues

The environmental issue in Asia has become very urgent, because the fresh water is running out. Moreover, Asia must share her water resource with many Asian countries and therefore have limitations on water resources. This must be addressed at regional level at least. The globalization and outsource have relocated many industries from developed countries to Asian countries. However, many out-of-date industries do more harm to our environment rather than do good. Here in Asia, many of these relocated factories are polluting Asia.

In this coming century, oil-rich countries could face a pretty sad situation if their valuable oil resource ran out. After, these countries would endure a post-oil economy, and the OPEC would cease to exist anymore. This global outcome would certainly not be an issue that concerns only one country, but would affect all oil-export countries and many are located in Asia. How can an economic model that is workable and profitable be created,? These oil-rich countries have been enjoying their oil revenue for so many years. Fifty years would still not be a sufficient enough time for these countries to search, study, and build a new economic model based on a mechanism different from the current one. This means that the oil-rich countries in Asia need to solve this problem for their own common interests.

There are indeed many issues that need to be addressed at an Asian level that close collaboration between Asian countries can solve. For example, Asia has to overcome issues with drug traffic, intellectual property, immigration, population, human rights, women traffic, and poverty.

1.2. SOLUTION

Before finding the solutions to solve these social-economic problems, the Asian people must first face the real problem as to whether or not we can address these problems as a united force for the whole Asia. Therefore, the question to put in front of Asian people is very simple. That is, whether to take action to find the way to address these problems at an Asian level or take no action. Our Asian history basically shows that our people seem to prefer no action and thus perhaps there is the cause of our sad history.

Some of these problems could vanish over time. No action perhaps is the best choice, for example the pollution led by the coal industry will vanish after the coal resource has been dug out. Still there are other problems, whose urgency becomes less pressing as time goes on and the choice of no action could also be a good. For example, family planning is not important for Japan, even the Japanese would like to have family planning and become less important as time goes on.

However, many of our Asian problems our people face would not automatically vanish in the foreseeing future. Even new problems may appear to be more important as time goes on. As an example there is the possibility of a post-oil economy. More importantly, Asian people need to seek solutions to stop the endless conflict and to control hotspots for potential wars in Asia. If we could solve these major problems, as well as a few of the minor problems, to give realistic timetable, within the next fifty or a hundred years, Asia would be able develop much faster. To have fewer conflicts, there would be less poverty, resulting in less drug trading that would lessen the threats in other parts of world. This is a great model for the future development in the Asian region.

However, there exist two major problems that still need to be fixed as quickly as possible. This is, the Asian people need to stop these endless conflicts because they claim so many lives of innocent people. Asian people must develop our economy fast because so many people are still living in poverty. It would be a great accomplishment if we could solve these two problems simultaneously.

The basic question remains: what is the reason why Asian people cannot join together? Under an Asian Union, its people can live peacefully and prosper. A workable solution to solve the various problems on an Asian level would theoretically create an Asian Union. Under the frame of an Asian Union, Asian countries could solve the problems together for their common interests and could compromise the unfavorable points between themselves.

A logical development for Asian history is to create an Asian Union, that could address the problems facing this Asian region. Now it is the time to work out such a plan, and analyze its suitability and discuss options.

It is very likely that there is no other part of the world which parallels Asia's situation. This region has social-economic complexity within its borders and major cultural differences. Asia perhaps is the most diverse region in the world.

The creation of an Asian Union would not be like the European Union where the social systems are quite similar among European countries. An Asian Union would not be a political union because the Asian countries within the region have very different political systems. Asia is comprised of just about every kind of social system thus far developed in human history. It is very unrealistic to expect to see a pan-Asian conference within world politics, where Asian people that have different political backgrounds could sit quietly together to discuss sensitive hot political issues. No, this is impossible. In politics, Asian countries are still potential enemies of each other!

Hence no one would expect to see an Asian constitution cross Asian countries. Clearly, any political union would probably end with endless discussions on trivial political issues. As a result, there would be no compromise reached for any political issue on an Asian level. Also do not expect to see an Asian Commission. We have seen the dysfunction of European Commission, and it is a rather bureaucratic institution. There would be the possibility of building an Asian Parliament but: could it pass any meaningful bill within a reasonable time? Consequently, an Asian Union as a political form would be a burden to Asian countries and its people; a waste of taxpayers money that would not be acceptable to Asian people.

In fact, it would be extremely costly to create any political union. For one might argue in a strange but practical way that the humans suffered so much during World War II, the resulting change in the political arena was that the League of Nations became the United Nations. Both political establishments dealt with global problems before and after World War II. Thus, a political Asian Union could form to deal with our current issues but would more than likely be short-lived.

Asian countries also cannot sit together quietly to discuss something related to religion. Many Asian conflicts are rooted from different religious beliefs, although each religion advocates living peacefully with people who have different beliefs. Therefore, we must give up on the idea that an Asian Union could be created under any frame of religion. This is to say, the Asian Union could not be a religious body; which is different from the European Union and the US, where a single religion dominates for the most part.

It is also not possible to create a military Asian Union, or see any form of a unified army at an Asian level. This is because Asia is very different from Europe and North America in terms of geographic characteristics and there are no easy connections inland cross much of the Asian continent. Moreover, the mobility for the navy, air force, and army in Asian countries would be relatively poor. apart from Japan and Israel, respectively. In addition, the military union would be impossible if a common political consent needed to be reached at an Asian level.

Thus, the only plausible solution for an Asian Union would be purely for an economic reason. The economic development is the only topic that almost all Asian countries can agree to talk about and is the great concern and interest for all Asian people. An economic agreement could be reached at an Asian level and the Asian people would have a uniform voice, perhaps.

Under such a circumstance, it is very possible to create an Asian Union as an economic union at an Asia level to promote the economic development within Asia, to enhance trade within Asia, and to eventually solve the other social-economic problems.

If no action is taken at an Asian level certain opportunities for a better future would be lost. Change is possible, as seen by the newly elected American President, new peaceful initiatives in Middle East, and the results of an economic slowdown worldwide. Asian people are aware that the 21st century will pass swiftly, and must face their regional problems.

1.3. FAVORABLE AND UNFAVORABLE POINTS

Although there are solutions to address the problems facing Asian people at an Asian level, the key factor is whether or not to take action. The question to ask then: can we find sufficient favorable points in order to take action? In plain words, we need to find how these actions would benefit governing parties in each Asian country. Simply because every governing party is mainly interested in holding power, as Chinese leader Mao Zedong had said, all we do is to maintain and consolidate power. This should be a starting point for taking action at an Asian level. Thus it is necessary to find out the favorable and unfavorable points for taking of action.

In principle, the solution to end the constant conflicts in Asia would be a benefit to all of Asia and some of the governing parties that are involved. Admittedly though, some of these governing parties do benefit from these endless conflicts. Yet to end the war conflicts is the hope and will of every ordinary Asian. Therefore, the hope would be that each governing party could be serious in finding a solution to end these conflicts; and would theoretically get the support of ordinary people. Unfortunately though, some party members would not know what to do without conflict.

In principle, this concept for an economic development would benefit actually all the governing parties, because it is common sense for the Asian people to hope to have a better life. However, this economic development is a real challenge for most Asian countries, because the Asian people lag far behind in the advances of world economics. This difficulty is clear when determining a economic model that is suitable for a particular Asian country, and to know the steps needed for economic development.

However, an Asian Union under an economic frame would help Asian countries. Although the Asian people already have several successful economic models, there would be a benefit for the countries to search for other economic solutions.

On the other hand, the unfavorable points have certain major obstacles, since the Asian countries tend to be internal-oriented countries and are afraid to open their borders to the outside world, and are reluctant to adopt many reforms.

Chapter 2

CONFLICT

The main obstacle concerning the creation of Asian Union is the endless conflicts within Asia. Over the years, there have been uncountable solutions for each conflict. However, some solutions only prolonged the conflicts when we look back at our past history. For instance, the UN resolutions in Middle East seemed to only prolong the existing conflict.

This means that we cannot simply root out various conflicts completely no matter what the best intentions might be because many of the proposed solutions to these conflicts are largely considered unsolvable problems inherited from history. History that involves many tangible causes for suffering and unjust conflicts. Honestly, there is not enough time to be able to explain an acceptable solution for all the wrongs done in the past.

However, the Asian people would have to address and minimize regional conflicts, in order to see change in the economic developments within Asia. Therefore, for any Asian Union to be possible a great part of our attention and effort should be to stop regional conflicts. This could be done by either economic development considerations or by diplomatic compromises. Perhaps, the ASEAN (Association of Southeast Asian Nations) could serve as an example. Although ASEAN had created a type of economic model in this regional, it was hardly heard on the international stage.

On the other hand, finding a solution to stop regional conflicts and cool these regional hotspots does not necessarily means that there must be intervention from other countries and some countries are entitled to intervene the internal affairs in the countries in question. The clear approach here must be to hold the attitude throughout that we should try to solve these problems rather than to create new problems.

The question raised here is: why we do not try to search for a way to let this conflict go? A non-fighting state is a thought, if we cannot completely eliminate the conflict from human society. Although, the idea of a non-fighting conflict state settlement does not actually solve the problem and is not the ideal solution, this approach at least prevents the endless bloodshed. This also provides the opportunity for a temporary peace with the possibility to promote economic development in the future. This should be considered as a sub-optimal solution.

Perhaps the best example of a common peace settlement in recent human history would be the Cold War, which in effect maintained the peace in Europe and North America after the end of World War II. The implication of the Cold War is that it created a balance after the conflict and resulted in a non-fighting state settlement. The positive effects were that it resulted in lasting peace and allowed for rapid economic development. As time goes by, the original cause for conflict does fade, as witnessed by the collapse of Soviet Union and the end of the Cold War.

If the two parties in conflict are somewhat equal either in size or military power, then the balanced conflict would be relatively stable and have less of a possibility of war. However, if the two sides of a conflict are very different in terms of military powers, it is hard to avoid the endless bloodshed. This would be considered an unbalanced conflict.

Thus, an optimistic approach to solving these endless conflicts in Asia at first would be to somehow transfer unbalanced conflicts into balanced conflicts. By hoping to create a short-term peace, perhaps then the initial reason for the conflict would become less important as time goes on, i.e. to persuade their reason for fighting and change their reasoning to pursue economic development.

The key point here sounds basic enough, transfer an unbalanced conflict into a balanced conflict. This cannot possibly be done by parties involved in conflict because the weak party in an unbalanced conflict has the disadvantage.. However, an external party outside conflict could be helpful for such a transformation and find a balance. It is the perfect role for the Asian Union.

2.1. TWO-PARTY CONFLICT

In general, most conflicts are two-party conflicts simply because there are two parties involved in a conflict. However, the problem is how to prevent the two-party conflict from becoming a real war that costs the lives of innocent people and destroys social wealth. The two-party conflict in Asia is quite common and it is either in form of civil war that happens within an Asian country or the conflict is between two Asian countries. Actually most Asian countries are neither very much interested in entering any two-party conflict in other Asian countries nor very much interested in introducing the third party into the conflict in their own countries.

2.1.1. Balanced Conflict

The Cold War between US and USSR is the best example for a balanced two-party conflict. No war occurred between these two major world powers for years, and no war happened between NATO countries and the Warsaw Treaty countries for years; even though each party was busy preparing for war. This balanced two-party conflict allowed the opportunity for rapidly economic development after World War II.

This means that a balanced two-party conflict is a tangible way to prevent a bloody war, when we cannot completely eliminate the other conflicts that arise in different ideologies. When the military in each party is equal, in theory, there is no clear victor, and those that are in conflict must seek alternatives.

This example reveals that a balanced two-party conflict can provide a short-term balance at worst, and may even create a relative long-term balance at best. Under a military balanced stand-off, the potential for a direct conflict makes both parties re-consider the catastrophic consequences possible. This common predicament led to create peace in Europe, aided economic competition and economic development to the benefit of ordinary people.

Actually, a balanced two-party conflict is not limited to a military conflict, but can also be attributed to ideology, economy, science, technology, and so on. During a considerable long post-war period, the US and USSR held the balance in most fields such economy, science, technology, and so on. No matter the people's preferences, the balanced two-party conflict helped to create peace after the war, and increased jobs, economic development, science, and technology.

Some idealists might suggest if a single social system could dominate the whole world then there might be fewer conflicts and wars. In fact, this peace has no guarantee for success, although a relatively long-term peace could be easily maintained within a single social system. Human history clearly shows there were always wars even during feudalism, and when most of the European countries had capitalism. History shows that this social system of the time could not prevent the wars. Thus a single uniform society system may not prevent conflicts and wars. In fact, a single uniform social system may collapse from internal chaos rather than external pressures.

Therefore, it can be argued that two opposing systems would be an important and necessary condition to create a balanced two-party conflict, as after World War II. Then the two social systems representatives were US and USSR. Nature and humans seem to favor duality like the balanced two-party conflicts. For example let us consider the following: positive and negative electrical charges, electron and proton (in the relative world of physics), good and bad, rich and poor, right and wrong, and the contrast of strong and weak. Another way to phrase it is that the world is defined by symmetry everywhere.

Therefore, the real solution is to create an balanced two-party conflict, that could maintain stability for two parties involved in the conflict. In short, the balanced two-party conflict is a way to maintain the peace rather than create peace. The incentive would be to promote economic development and to advance human, specifically Asian society.

If we look for the two-part conflicts in Asia, too many exist. We have the potential conflicts between North Korea and South Korea, between India and Pakistan, between Iran, US, and Israel, the continued conflict between Israel and Palestine, and the civil war in Sri Lanka, etc. Almost all these conflicts are due to the hostility against a completely opposite social system, or oppositing concepts, religions, territorial claims, etc.

Among these conflicts in Asia, the balanced two-party conflict can only be clearly seen between India and Pakistan. In the past, the conflict between both Koreas was a balanced two-party conflict with the support from the US and Soviet Union respectively. Similarly, the conflict between Israel and Egypt was a balanced two-party conflict that ultimately led to a peace deal between both parties [6].

Along this line of thought, the unbalanced two-party conflicts in Asia provide the opportunities for the proposed Asian Union to approach to these conflicts by finding a means to transfer each unbalanced two-party conflict into a managable balanced two-party conflict.

2.1.2. Unbalanced Conflict

By clear contrast, the unbalanced two-party conflict is a probable factor that can lead to a war, and is a very unstable peace even if a temporary peace exists between two parties. In Asia, all the endless bloodshed could be attributed to unbalanced two-party conflicts.

History shows that all the colonization wars could be classified as unbalanced two-party conflicts. The first and second Sino-Japanese wars were unbalanced two-party conflicts, not only because Japan had a stronger military power, but Japan was more advanced in ideology, economy, science, and technology. An unbalanced two-party conflict would be relatively easy for the stronger party to become the clear victor.

It is very natural to consider that many two-party conflicts begin as an imbalance where there is one weaker party and one stronger party and each of them are at different stages of social development. Sometimes there is a huge imbalance between contrasting societies; in such a case, the result of conflict is predictable, as shown by the colonization wars. Therefore, an unbalanced two-party conflict is more likely to be created by human desires.. This is to say, humans deliberately and intentionally create unbalanced two-party conflicts that have caused endless hatred, bloodshed and a dominant victor.

Recent history shows that under a balanced two-party conflict between major two superpowers during Cold War, each superpower tried hard to initiate an unbalanced conflict outside Europe and North America, i.e., Korean War, Vietnam war, Cuba, Chile, etc. This means that the powerful countries, when they cannot attack each other, would do their best to find a place, where they would either create an unbalanced two-party conflict or transfer a balanced two-party conflict into an unbalanced two-party conflict through military training, military and economic aids, and other methods. This endangers the world in many ways.

On the other hand, the unbalanced two-party scenerio has the potential possibility that the stronger party could readily attack the weaker party;, but there is always the possibility that a weaker party may choose to attack the stronger party firstly. Although seemingly illogical, the fact remains for example Japan attacked the US during World War II. In recent Asian history, we could see that the current Palestine-Israel conflict and Sri Lanka civil war are the typical unbalanced two-party conflict. However, the weaker party still frequently attacks the stronger party no matter the loss suffered. These described desperate attacks from the weaker parties against stronger parties in an unbalanced two-party conflict could merely suggest that the weaker party sees little hope for the future. Asian people must somehow try to provide the hope by find ways to alter these two-party conflicts in Asia. Isn't time to stop our pain and suffering?

In short, an unbalanced two-party conflict had benefits for the stronger party in history, but now neither the stronger nor the weaker party would benefit. The weaker party would only suffer more than the stronger party during a conflict. An unbalanced two-party conflict can cause a war between two parties and instead of peace, there is only endless pain for each party involved in conflict.

Therefore, for the sake of peace in Asia, we should do our best to eliminate any unbalanced two-party conflict in Asia.

2.1.3. Third Party's Role in Two-party Conflict

For any two-party conflict the role of third party is in fact very simple. This is that the choice of the third party can either transfer an unbalanced two-party conflict into a balanced two-party conflict; or transfer a balanced two-party conflict into an unbalanced two-party conflict.

The Taiwan problem has been a balanced two-party conflict for more than a half a century. In fact, China would not attack Taiwan because the treaty with the US guarantees the safety of Taiwan. This means that the involvement of US transferred an unbalanced two-party conflict into a balanced two-party conflict. Although the US government perhaps initially had not planned to transfer an unbalanced two-party conflict into a balanced two-party conflict, their involvement ensured peace for both sides of Taiwan Strait.

Cuba is another case in point, where an unbalanced two-party conflict existed between Cuba and the US and this situation became a balanced two-party conflict attributed to strong support from Soviet Union to Cuba. Years after this balanced two-party conflict, the US has no more direct conflict with Cuba. It is obvious that this balanced two-party conflict does not exist any more since the collapse of Soviet Union, however, the US already has no strong intention to invade Cuba. This could be an effective example that there are ways that reasoning can change a conflict; the situation can change as time goes on.

This suggests an interesting role that the third party plays to alter a region from an unbalanced two-party conflict and through diplomacy transfer an unbalanced two-party conflict into a balanced two-party conflict. After the third party's disengagement,, even a balanced two-party conflict has the potential to become an unbalanced two-party conflict; yet if enough time passes as in one or possibly two generations; the conflict often is then more indirect and would have little possibility of war.

On the other hand, the involvement of third party could also transfer a balanced two-party conflict into an unbalanced two-party conflict. The possibility of war and bloodshed can occur when a balanced two-party conflict has no solution without the involvement of a strong third party.

This suggests the only way to balance any two-party conflict either by the introduction of a third party or by the prevention of the involvement of third party. These decisions could be reached either through the pressure of internal politics on the governing third party or through the pressure from an international organization. In this context it preferably would be an Asian Union.

Another fact related to the two-party conflict with the involvement of third party in Asia is that the third party generally supports a country at national level rather than supports a particularly political party under national level. For example, the US government does not particularly concern which party is in control of South Korea, Taiwan, or Israel, etc. This approach prevents the involvement of third party from the governing party in the country that may have a close relationship with the third party. To illustrate, the Chinese support for Cambodia was mainly related to King Norodom Sihanouk and Khmer Rouge, this support became null with the change in governing party in Cambodia. This also means that it would be difficult to build a puppet government supported by a third party in Asia.

At any rate, Asian people should think twice as to whether there is really a need for an introduction of third party to transfer a balanced two-party conflict in Asia into an unbalanced two-party conflict in Asia.

2.2. THREE- OR MULTI-PARTY CONFLICT

Another interesting situation would be three- or multi-party conflict in a small region. This could arguably be a solution to these endless conflicts, as learned from engineering that at least three points can make a system stable.

A three- or multi-party conflict is by no means that any party in an existing conflict opens a new front to confront another enemy as Nazi Germany began to fight the Soviet Union before a decisive victory over the

UK. Japan also began to fight the US before there was a decisive victory over China during World War II, but can be still considered as two-party conflict.

The real three- or multi-party conflict is when each party has enough reason to fight with any other party in this three- or multi-party conflict. The three- or multi-party conflict would be characteristic of a civil war in Asia, where many warlords fight each other in order to seize the national power.

In most cases, a three- or multi-party conflict could provide a temporary stability, a relatively peaceful time for economic development, because a balance is relatively easy to be created in three- or multi-party conflict than in a two-party conflict. In Chinese history, three kingdoms (220 – 280 AD) could be a typical three-party conflict [7], where each party had sufficient reasons to attack any other party and also had sufficient reasons to unite and compromise any second party to attack the third party.

In three- or multi-party conflict, the balance or unbalance between any two parties becomes less important, but the importance is how two weaker parties can find a common basis to defend them or to attack a stronger party. A three- or multi-party conflict can also be interpreted in the context of democratic elections, and thus would be a very common phenomenon within a democratic country. However, a three- or multi-party conflict is a rare case at regional or international level among countries. Even a three-party conflict is unlikely to appear at regional or international level; needless to mention how unlikely for a multi-party conflict at regional or international level.

Hence the appearance of a three-party conflict at regional level should be considered a great opportunity provided by providence, and this type of opportunity should not be missed because it has a real opportunity to create a temporary peace among all the parties involved in conflict.

Actually, a three-party conflict now appears likely in the Middle East. It will require a great courage to utilize this opportunity to create a possible peace in Middle East. The previous conflict in Middle East was never a three-party conflict, but always either a balanced two-party conflict supported by US and Soviet Union or an unbalanced two-party conflict supported by US alone.

2.4. IMPLICATION FOR ASIA

All these considersations mean that for peace in Asia, and to stop the endless conflicts in Asia; the Asian people should do their best to transfer unbalanced two-party conflicts in Asia into balanced two-party conflicts. This may provide the opportunity for economic development. Then, we can only hope that the reason for conflicts would perhaps fade step-by-step, and thereafter these two-party conflicts could be solved through a more peaceful means for good.

Due to the unbalanced economic development in Asia, a two-party conflict frequently leads to the involvement of a stronger third party, or even two third parties. Their involvement transfers the existed two-party conflict to either a balanced two-party conflict as Taiwan or an unbalanced two-party conflict as civil war in Sri Lanka. A regional war, bloodshed, and loss of life of innocent people often follow.

A realistic approach to endless conflicts in Asia is that (i) we need the introduction of third party to create a balanced two-party conflict, to reach a temporary peace if there is no third party involved previously, (ii) or we need the introduction of a new third party to support the weaker side in an unbalanced two-party conflict. If there has already been a third party involved on stronger side, to create symmetry for a balanced two-party conflict, (iii) or we need to persuade the third party to exit from an unbalanced two-party conflict.

The Asian history shows that a strong third party frequently comes from a country outside Asia. On the other hand, sometimes a third party could come from an Asian country if the third party has a close proximity to the two-part conflict, or the third party has direct interests, as for example the civil war in Sri Lanka.

The balance is impossible for any unbalanced two-party conflict unless the third party can support the weaker party in this unbalanced two-party conflict. This third party must be a major power, whose military should overwhelm the stronger party in this two-party conflict.

At an international level, the only third party that has enough military and economic power to be involved in any two-party conflict in Asia is the United

States of America. When looking at most conflicts in the world at this time, there is no major power in the world that has the ability to be involved as an opposite party against the party supported by the US in two-party conflict in the world. Needless to say, this is with respect to any two-party conflicts in Asia.

In this social economic world, no matter the preference of the Asian people, the endorsement from the US government in unbalanced two-party conflicts in Asia is a key factor to stop the endless bloodshed in Asia. To reduce tension in a two-party conflict, and to produce a relatively stable Asia for economic development, only a major power possesses that kind of influence.

At this moment, no Asian country has the ability to change the influence that the US government has for so many years. However, a proposed Asian Union could persuade the US government to play a peaceful and constructive role in Asia. On the other hand, a proposed Asian Union could transfer an unbalanced two-party conflict in Asia into a balanced two-party conflict and bring peace to the region. The US government may not be interested in this two-party conflict. Still Asian countries should endorse the involvement of US in this region, because most Asian countries do not have the ability to bring about needed changes for the region.

Chapter 3

EAST ASIA

East Asia perhaps is the number one place in the world with an extremely high potential for a regional war to occur because there exists an unbalanced two-party conflict since the collapse of Soviet Union. In this same region, not long before this, a balanced two-party conflict existed between both Koreas at the end of Korean War.

On the other hand, East Asia has one of the most active economies in the world which includes China, Hong Kong, Japan, South Korea, and Taiwan. Theoretically, East Asia has a good potential to create an economic cluster, where the economic powers could establish much closer ties and even consider the adoption of a multi-currency momentary system.

However, East Asia is also a place, where strong distrusts and mistrusts exist between countries due to several reasons; for example, a duel currency system is unlikely to be applied equally to China and Japan because of their history of distrust.

Yet, every effort should be made to integrate the economy in East Asia. For promoting closer economic relationships among these East Asia countries would be one plausible solution to prevent the occurrence of potential disasters in East Asia. Any solution aimed to help reduce the tension in this highly dangerous region would be a benefit to all of East Asia.

3.1. NORTH KOREA

3.1.1. Problem

Although there are many problems in East Asia, as an example the problems that exist between China and Taiwan; the most pressing problem is perhaps North Korea. It is extremely likely that North Korea will be the next hotspot in the world. Especially for the next generation of leaders in North Korean where significant challenges will certaintly be faced, particularly in Northeast Asia. In fact, no one knows what North Korea would do? This uncertainty for the future has many aspects. Although it is said that uncertain retaliation is more efficient than certain retaliation [8], this uncertainty as to what the new North Korea leaders would do or if their leaders would retaliate against the rest of world; makes people nervous and uneasy. Let us assume several probabilities related to the North Korea for the near future.

The first possibility: would the next generation leaders be over confident and have a big ambition. Of course, the major ambition for North Korea would be uniting with South Korea. Thus, North Korean would likely conduct more missile tests, and would speed up a program to develop a nuclear arsenal.

In the past, the two-party conflict between North Korea and South Korea was balanced by the involvement of two third parties, the US and Soviet Union. The peace produced by this balanced two-party conflict had been maintained over the years until very recently. By the collapse of Soviet Union, this balanced two-party conflict became a unbalanced two-party conflict. History suggests, as argued in the previous chapter, the unbalanced two-party conflict is an unstable phase that might turn into a war, especially when North Korea feels her existence is in danger. Although, as a weaker party in an unbalanced two-party conflict, North Korea could desperately attack the stronger party firstly. The threat for North Korea to use nuclear weapons to prevent any further involvement by a third party could start a new Korean war.

From a Japanese viewpoint,the fast development of a nuclear program by North Korea would endanger Japan and her interests. This situation would be intolerable for Japan. History clearly shows that Japan would not hesitate to conduct preemptive attacks if it considered it necessary. For example, the

Russo-Japanese war from 1904 to 1905 was initiated when the Japanese navy attacked the Russian Far East fleet at Port Arthur before their Declaration of War reached the Russian government [9]. Another more profound example that represents Japanese characteristics is the attack on Pearl Harbor. Thus, there is a strong possibility for Japan to attack North Korea if provoked. . Considering the size of North Korea, such an attack by Japan would be quite easy. This simulation of an attack on the North Korea and its nuclear establishment has no doubt been rehearsed many times within Japan. However, the Japanese may consider there would be less of a possibility for a severe consequence by their preemptive attack, if one analyzes their preemptive attacks during World War II.

Thus, if Japan were to attack a nuclear facility in North Korea, this would have an extremely severe result. First, a nuclear pollution threat would exist in Northeast Asia. This would be more severe than the nuclear accident in Chernobyl because the population density in Asia is much higher than in Europe. This would also lead to other desperate attacks, such as from North Korea on South Korea, and then perhaps Japan and the US. As a result, North Korea more than likely would be defeated by South Korea, Japan, and the US. Yet, there would be little possibility of any involvement by the Chinese army in this new Korean war, unless the war entered into the Chinese territory. China would generally consider this type of war as an internal affair. In fact, at the beginning of the previous Korean War some Chinese leaders considered it as a civil war [10] and did not support the Chinese army to be involved.

The second possibility to consider would be if the next generation of leaders are weaker than the previous two generations of leaders, which would cause frequent power changes in North Korea. For this scenario in such a deteriorated economy, the only consequence would be coups with unknown consequences. This would not be a positive prospective for everyone, because it would clearly increase the difficulty to predict the behavior of North Korea and keep other countries nervous and alert. This means that each party has a direct interest in North Korea, and hopes to see a stable North Korea rather than an unpredictable and unstable North Korea. The best hope for global peace would be to see North Korea to return to the international community.

The third possibility to consider is if nothing changed in North Korea, although this probably is the most likely case it would be a slow process of suicide. This approach may lead North Korea to go in the path of the sub-Sahara countries. It would be a reasonable possibility that the economy would collapse in North Korea, because its economy could not bear the burden of long-term high oil price, and massive military spending, etc. On the other hand, this theoretical collapse of North Korea's economy would lead to unpredictable consequences for all of East Asia.

3.1.2. Who Has Interests

Actually, North Korea is not a country, which plays an important role at international stage. North Korea has almost no regional or world entitlements, however her future is directly related to the interests of South Korea, China, Japan, Russia, and the US. In this view, the position of North Korea is very particular, where any solution related to North Korea needs the involvement of five countries to obtain a peaceful compromise.

3.1.3. Solution

All three possibilities would destabilize the Northeast Asia and possibly even lead to a new Korean war in the future, and thus we should do our best to avoid.

An important, yet possible solution for the North Korea problem is to integrate the North Korea's economy into the Chinese economy. This solution would stabilize North Korea, and reduce the threat of war between North Korea and Japan, between North Korea and South Korea with US. This could be considered as an alternative way for a new third party to be introduced into this unbalanced two-party conflict between North Korea and South Korea.

In general, the economic mechanism that exists in North Korea is very similar to the current Chinese economic mechanism. In particular, the North Korea economic model is still widely applied in Northeast China, Thus it would be an easy way for North Korea to go, and become part of the Chinese economic cluster.

If this would happen, North Korea and China could adopt both currencies in both North Korea and Northeast China. This step would lead to an open border between China and North Korea, allow for free trade between the two countries, and free movement for people between these countries.

This could possibly be called a win-win situation. North Korean people would have the ability to come to China for work or trade their goods with Chinese people, and the Chinese would directly invest into North Korea. Educational level in North Korea is in fact very high and would indeed be a benefit for Chinese investment in North Korea.

This possibility could promote a rapid development in North Korea's economy, and substantially reduce the possibility of destabilization in Northeast Asia. For Chinese, who shares their border, would enjoy more business, more services and even more tourism. This would also be an important step for the development of Northeast China that lags far behind Southeast China.

The prolonged problem of illegal immigrants from North Korea to China would diminish if North Korean people could freely pass the border and bring back money they earn from China.

The first stage of the proposal, South Korea, Japan, and the US should pay China for her effort to stabilize Northeast Asia and reduce the possibility of war. Another possibility would to create a North Korea development bank funded by South Korea, Japan and the US to cooperate in the investment of North Korea.

This step would lead to further integration of the economy in Northeast Asia and to Sino-Korea-Japan economic cluster. Three economic giants could contribute to a great ideal concept that is benefical toward world development, and could serve as a model for the integration of various economies within East Asia. And this economic model can promote the reduction of regional tension.

3.1.4. Who Gains

This proposed solution would be great gain for the leadership in North Korea. The people living in North Korea would be happy for the fast economic development, and have less military duties. Also a strong Chinese currency would provide North Korea with the opportunity for international trade. This also would reduce the possibility of attack on North Korea by Japan. At an international stage, the image of North Korea would change significantly with the possibility to attract more investments. North Korea is the only place in East Asia yet to be developed.

However, the real and clear fact is that no one really wishes to see a united Korea, neither North Korea nor South Korea. For North Korea, a united Korea not only means the collapse of her social system. Also, it means that the leaders in North Korea could not win any election in a united Korea, which would be hard for them to accept.

For South Korea, a united Korea would be like a united Germany with endless pain and trouble. In the best scenario, a united Korea would be the dream for the next generation, and even this somewhat unrealistic. In theory though this proposed solution would be a gain for South Korea, if South Korea could avoid the difficulties that happened in Germany. On the positive side, South Korea could heavily invest in North Korea. The worst scenario here is that South Korea, Japan, and the US would lose nothing, but would gain free trade between China and North Korea.

This proposed solution would also be a great gain for Japan. North Korea under this Chinese economic cluster would reduce the possibility of war, induced by air strike on North Korea's nuclear facility. Although no one would suggest that the nuclear facility in North Korea would be under Chinese control, the attention of leadership of North Korea would move away from military development to an economic development.

This proposed solution would be the gain for the US, because of the worry the US has concerning the nuclear program in North Korea. If the North Korea economy would integrate into Chinese economy, this region would certainly be more peaceful.

For Russia, this would be the gain because the current focus in Russia is more internally-oriented. Russia has little interest in North Korea other than the hopeful view for a more stable North Korea.

Another natural development in this proposal would be to build an economic cluster with both Koreas and Japan. If so, this cluster would be the biggest free economic zone in the world. Let us consider an East Asia economic cluster. This could be possible since these four countries have a similar culture with common history that stems from the traditional Chinese civilization. In theory, their language and culture barriers are comparatively small for these three countries.

The potential difficulty would be that Japan and South Korea are afraid of economic immigrants from North Korea and China; although the population of Japan shrinks year by year. In this aspect, South Korea and Japan could be possible losers although they can impose a limited number of free visas.

3.2. Mongolia

There is no two-party conflict either between China and Mongolia or between Russia and Mongolia. The geographical location and population size of Mongolia make the involvement of a third party into this non-conflict region less of an interest. Although some leaders of old school ambition still show an infrequent but often temporary interest in Mongolia. This political game in this region is easy to settle.

The problem for Mongolian people is mainly related to their economic development, because their economy has little connection with interests by outside world. This means that no major party has strong economic or military interests in Mongolia.

Since the collapse of the Soviet Union,, the Mongolians have yet to find a way to integrate into the world. This was demonstrated when US President Bush visited there in 2005.

Another problem is that the current Russia is not very much interested in Mongolia, though there once was a close tie between these two countries in history. In fact, the current Russia shows little interest in the Central Asia too, simply because Central Asia and Mongolia have what Russia already has.

Actually, since Mongolia is a landlocked country, it has a good opportunity to build a better economic relationship with the Chinese economy. The language barrier between Mongolia and the Inner Mongolia of China would be minimal, if not zero. Still the population size of Mongolia would not cause any economic hardship for the Chinese living in Inner Mongolia of China. This is a very good starting point for both China and Mongolia, with the expectation to allow their currencies to circulate in both countries.

This would be possible not only on an economic level, but the natural condition between Mongolia and Inner Mongolia in China is very similar and Mongolia needs Chinese investment. China realistically is the nearest resource for Mongolia. Thus, this economic cluster would be quite easy to build up.

This solution would be good for both parties, because Mongolia would benefits from China's investments and the Inner Mongolia in China would create free trade between Mongolia and other parts of China there by providing much needed services.

History has shown that once Mongolians possessed amazing mobile speed, which enabled Genghis Khan to build the Mongol Empire. Now Mongolians need the speed for an economic development through this opportunity to create a better relationship with other countries in East Asia.

3.3. TAIWAN

The current situation between Mainland China and Taiwan is a balanced two-party conflict with the involvement of third party. The Taiwan problem is indeed too hard to be solved by military means. In some sense, because of its long historical past, Taiwan now has fewer options to solve current problems.

Strictly speaking, this Taiwan problem only has direct interest for Mainland China and Taiwan. Thus, here lies the two-party conflict. Although US has an agreement with Taiwan, this agreement does not give many military and economic gains to the US. The value for the US government is strategic.

Therefore, clearly any solution related to Taiwan needs to also consider the US. Even so, the problem is still in deadlock. Any military solutions could leave both sides as losers. If China would attack Taiwan, even without the US involvement, the attacks and counterattacks would lead to the unimaginable loss of life and wealth. This is simply because the distance between Mainland China and Taiwan is too short to have any efficient defense. The direct consequence would most likely be the stagnation of economy on both sides, if not worse. So this obvious solution would result in two losers.

The application of applying a Hong Kong model toward Taiwan means the disarmament of Taiwan. Here, the clear loser would be Taiwan, and thus Taiwan would not accept this solution.

The direct return of Taiwan to Mainland China, although impossible, still suggests that both sides would be the losers. There are few government positions available for Taiwan officers in Mainland China. On the other hand, Taiwan would be afraid for the flood of job-hunters from Mainland China.

The only hope is that both sides still desire to see a united China, and the best solution would be an increase in the economic integration between Mainland China and Taiwan.

Actually the current situation is lightly in favor of Mainland China, because the Mainland China is out pacing Taiwan. This difference in their speed of economic development; Taiwan may become more isolated on an international level. Since the US is only the interested party her attention and concern would be less for Taiwan.

Chapter 4

WEST ASIA

It is out of question to consider that West Asia is a place where there are too many conflicts to deal with. It is reasonable to consider it as a place where the solution has many difficulties that are simultaneously related to many countries. The fact that there is no large-scale peace deal suggests that any peace agreement is more likely to be reached between two countries. Many countries have seen peace agreements in this region, like between Israel and Jordan [11], and between Israel and Egypt [6].

For the situation in West Asia, more exactly, in the Middle East, it has been in a deadlock for at least a couple of years. Before new situations can appear in the region, this deadlock needs to be solved. In fact, this region can easily build an economic cluster faster than any other place in Asia. This region is dominated by a single religion and a limited number of languages. Still, the economic pattern in this region is very similar, and the oil exports for these countries provide plenty of money. Besides, the natural surroundings are similar in this region; therefore the West Asian economic cluster with a multi-currency system, free trade and open borders for people is possible among all Asian countries.

A plausible solution for this region in particular is: if each government can have an internal political gain after reaching the compromise; since these conflicts require a complex compromise. Interestingly, the free election mechanisms in these conflict-troubled countries such as Israel, Palestine, Iran, and Iraq are relatively effective compared with other Asian countries.

4.1. ISRAELI-PALESTINE CONFLICT

The Israeli-Palestine conflict is really an unbalanced two-party conflict even though there is involvement of third party, the US. This case is much worse, since this unbalanced two-party conflict cannot be brought into a balanced two-party conflict by means of introducing a new third party. The real fact is that currently no country in Middle East, or in the world has sufficient power to confront Israel and her supporter, the US. The Soviet Union did perhaps at one time, yet there is no other country has any real intention to do so.

For this endless conflict, as Sun Tzu said [12]: "You must not fight too often with one enemy, or you will teach him all your art of war." In this Israeli-Palestine conflict, each party now is quite familiar with their opposing strategy and tactics that the other party uses. More than that, each party also is very familiar with all the possible conditions set for a peace talk. Hence, all these are obstacles. These issues are the real problem that prevents the end of this long-term and unbalanced two-party conflict. New ideas and concepts are desperately needed for any initiative for peaceful settlement in this conflict.

The first question to ask now is: who has a real direct interest in the Israeli-Palestine conflict?; and who can gain if an agreement of peace is reached? History shows that the leaders in Middle East conflict-troubled countries have gained a lot after reaching an agreement or accord on peace. Hope for a lasting peace for this region in particular showed promise, for example by Yitzhak Rabin and Ariel Sharon.

This is the true basis for peace in the region, or at least a serious peace talk. Arguably the final goal for either Israel or Palestine is the economic development. Even if it was possible to destroy their opponent in this unbalanced two-party conflict, the fact is that neither Israel nor Palestine could destroy each other.

In fact recently, a nice possibility can arise for a temporary peace. This possibility requires great courage, a new concept on definition, patience, and an effective compromise.

The solution would recognize the Hamas government. Nevertheless the Hamas movement would gain dramatically from the recognition, which seems to be extremely unhappy for the US and Israel. The Hamas government has been defined as a terrorism organization. However, for this internationally political gain, there is a great and good possibility that the Hamas government would radically soften her attitude toward Israel and other related issues in Middle East. The recognition would really be the greatest dream for Hamas government in this troubled land. Similarly, just as China had desperately hoped to be recognized after creation of the People's Republic of China.

However, the most important point here is the recognition of Hamas government would lead to a three-party conflict in this troubled Middle East. This is to say that Israel, the Palestine government in West Bank, and the Hamas government in Gaza could construct the three-party conflict. Among these three parties, each party would have her own reason to go against any of the other two parties. This would be the first, if not the last opportunity to create a three-party conflict in Middle East, and an extremely rare opportunity for a temporary peace in Middle East. In the worst scenario, hopefully the US and Israel governments would not let this opportunity pass due to their ideological definition that they do not talk with terrorist group.

It is hard to create a balanced two-party conflict in Middle East, since the collapse of Soviet Union. Therefore a possible and important solution in Middle East is to change the unbalanced two-party conflict between Palestine and Israel into a three- or multi-party conflict. This would create a short-term balance and peace in Middle East.

In particular, the would-be-newly-recognized Hamas government would be more interested in the power struggle with the Palestine authority in West Bank. However the hope that Hamas in the power struggle with the Palestine authority in West Bank would be effectively separated by Israel. Thus, the civil war between Hamas government in Gaza and Palestine authority in West Bank may therefore be completely impossible. On the other hand, the Palestine people would be influenced by the achievements either by Hamas government in Gaza or by Palestine government in West Bank. A party that the regional people would vote for in the next election would result in a peaceful and economic competition between Hamas government in Gaza or Palestine government in West Bank for coming years, even decades.

This would create the real power balance between Gaza and West Bank. On the other hand, Israel's government would not consider any proposal to have the peace talk with a single authority either from Gaza or West Bank, but would treat them equally. Otherwise, this balanced three-party conflict would slide into an unbalanced two-party conflict with the possibility of new bloodshed after reaching a peace agreement with either Gaza or West Bank.

For their internal interests in this geographically separated power struggle, both authorities in Gaza and West Bank must soften their attitude towards Israel. In order to attract more financial aid from the moderate Arab countries, European Union, and the US, the Hamas should concentrate on economic issues in both Gaza and West Bank to obtain the people's support. After one or two generations of stability in the region, peace could be reached through the integration of economy between Gaza and Israel and between Israel and West Bank.

The compromising condition for Hamas seems to be simple, that is to avoid an attack on Israeli soil. On the other hand, the compromising condition for Israel seems to be simple as well; that is, the recognition of Hamas on an international level. If both sides can compromise these two conditions, then the problem between West Bank government and Hamas government would be more significant. Meanwhile, there is no way for the West Bank government to overthrow the Hamas government in Gaza. There is also no way for the Hamas government to overthrow the West Bank government in West Bank because they are efficiently separated by Israel. Now, the only obstacle would be to avoid an attack on Israeli soil, and the willingness to talk with the Hamas government.

Yet, one cannot compare the separation of Palestine by Gaza and West Bank with the separation of Pakistan in the last century because this is a totally different case.

The current policy held by US and Israel has no future, since this is based on an ideological policy. History shows that any ideological policy could not solve a long-existing political problem. No dialogue with a terrorist group is the policy, and limits the political options, as well as limits the US and Israel themselves. For Hamas government, the biggest hope would be to be recognized world-wide For such a purpose, the Hamas government has the possibility to compromise. The US and Israel would always have the option to cut their relationship with Hamas if they want.

In general, it would take years to reach the level of peace where there are completely no attacks on Israeli soil from Gaza because no government or organization can prevent a random event; as seen recently by the international navy power that cannot prevent the pirates in East Africa. Therefore, it may need to distinguish a systematical attack on Israeli soil by an organization from a random attack on Israel soil by a single group composed of several people. In the latter case, a random attack could become somewhat tolerant if the Hamas government would seriously deal with such an attack.

Meanwhile, a punishment war is also not solution, that actually uses the taxpayers' money to conduct a war;, then again uses taxpayers' money to award private construction companies for reconstruction. Clearly, the punishment method is not the best solution.

There is a possibility that the Palestine authority in West Bank could go against the recognition of Hamas in Gaza by Israel. This would not be decisive for getting the internal support from both Hamas and authority in West Bank to engage in economic development, which would provide an opportunity for Israel to integrate these three economies together.

On the other hand, the Palestine authority in West Bank could consider herself as a loser if the international community would recognize the Hamas. However, the feeling could be well compensated by the economic aid package from the US, European Union, and Israel. Besides, the authority in West Bank would consider this deal as gain because the Hamas government was also legitimately elected.

A more favorable situation would be that this three-party conflict would extend to a multi-party conflict in Middle East to include the balanced two-party conflict in Lebanon. This would freeze the hotspots and hostile activity in Middle East, although this means that Israel would eventually recognize

Hezbollah. Nevertheless, Israel government would gain internally and politically as shown by Yitzhak Rabin and Ariel Sharon.

If this opportunity happened, where the Hamas would control both Gaza and West Bank or the current Palestine authority in West Bank would control both Gaza and West Bank, then it would take many years to have another three-party conflict in this troubled region.

4.2. IRAN NUCLEAR PROGRAM

At this moment, the Iranian government has no power to strike any country with her nuclear power. Also the Iranian government dares not strike any country with nuclear weapons. In fact, no country dares to strike any other country using the nuclear weapons since the end of World War II.

However, a country with strong military establishment in her past, and now with plenty of money could naturally have new ambitions in this world.

The real fact is that the current Iran has only a few options: (i) Towards south and east, Iran would affect the US interest in this region. Any serious conflict with the US would draw Iranian economy back decades, because it is the tradition for the US air force to destroy infrastructures in any country in a war. (ii) Towards southwest, Iran would face Israel, which has a far better and experienced air force than Iran has. On the other hand, the current conflict between Iran, US, and Israel is not a three-party conflict, but a two-party conflict with the involvement of third party. This has a danger to lead to war.

From another point of view, the conflict in Lebanon becomes a balanced two-party conflict with the involvement of third party by Iran and keeps Lebanon in peace. Still due to the existence of Iran, the conflict between Israel and Syria becomes a balanced two-party conflict. These two balanced two-party conflicts in Middle East are necessary and important; otherwise all the Middle East would be aflame with endless bloodshed. It is therefore a hope that neither Israel nor the US nor Iran does anything to unbalance them.

Although North Korea sets an example for Iran to pursue a nuclear program, the proposed solution for North Korea is not suitable for Iran because there is no power that is larger than Iran in this region. In this view,

Iran would be an undisputable power in this region, which is very suggestive, because Iran might not need to be armed to the teeth or in a hurry to develop a nuclear program.

If Iran is an undisputable power in this region, and its current approach is to develop a nuclear program to confront the south, which represents the interests of US and Israel, this would not be very wise. This may directly lead to a dangerous conflict. The Iranian government could actually consider an option to develop towards North, and build a better relationship with Turkey.

This possible solution would draw the Iranian interests from south to north and hopefully create a better relationship with Turkey. The possible solution would be to build an oil or gas export pipeline from Iran to Europe through Turkey. The change of focus for Iran from south to north would reduce further tension in Middle East, to reduce the existing tensions between Syria and Israel,or Lebanon and Israel, where a new three-party conflict could be built among Lebanon factions and Israel afterwards.

The problem now is what the Iranian government would consider for such a strategic transform in this regional focus from south to north. Nevertheless, the Iranian government would do it if this option would be considered as a gain. In fact, this would be a big gain not only for the Iranian government but also for the outside world.

This proposal would be helpful: (i) the tension between Iran and the US, as well as Iran and Israel, also Iran and Europe would reduce, (ii) the chance of striking from Israel and the US on Iranian nuclear facility would reduce, (iii) the Iranian government would get more support from moderate Iranians, and (iv) the Iranian government would have a far better relationship with the US after the building of pipeline to export oil and gas through Turkey.

This solution would also be a gain for the US government, not only because this solution reduces the chance of direct conflict with Iran, but also because this solution leaves the opportunity for the US troop to completely withdraw from Iraq in the future.

This solution would also be a gain for Israel, because Israel would have less of a worry to open a second front in north and could concentrate on peace deal with Palestine.

Therefore, this solution really needs the endorsements from European countries and the US.

Historically, Iran was a more European-oriented country; now it is time to focus from troubled Middle East to Europe, where her economic interests would lie in the future. Moreover, the human history in Middle East does not show any nation or country can really profit or gain anything from this troubled region besides pouring money and lives into a continued struggle. This lesson should be suggested the non-Middle East country that has an interest to be involved in this troubled region.

4.3. AFGHANISTAN WAR

Although the geographical location of Afghanistan is said to be in Central Asia [13], this country almost has no business with Central Asia. In a broad sense as having a role in the world, no one understands and knows the real reason of why this landlocked country draws so much attention from so many world powers.

Currently there are clear solutions to the Afghanistan war, but the results are that the US led NATO troops cannot completely destroy the Taliban in a limited time with limited forces.

The US policy where the government is unwilling to talk or negotiate with the Taliban leaves only one option. The Taliban must fight and die. However, this approach may require far more US troops and NATO troops to fight and use their logistic resources. It is almost impossible to convince Americans and Europeans to allow the US and NATO governments to send more troops into the Afghanistan. Therefore, this war is the war without an obvious dominant force, the US and NATO troops are superior in weaponry and movement, but the Taliban are good surviving in the mountains and are able to get support from local residents. There is a possible way for this war to end; a decision by a US president to change the course in Afghanistan. A withdrawal of US and NATO troops could leave Afghanistan in chaos, a multi-party conflict among various warlords, who are now sitting quietly and are waiting for that time to come.

Another difficulty is the complete unknown about the power structure of the Taliban. The CIA has had their difficulties.

Currently there is no other organized group in Afghanistan as strong as Taliban. In a way, the Taliban are controlling the war. This is the fact no matter if the international community agrees or not. Without US troop and NATO troops, the conflict between Afghanistan government and Taliban would become an unbalanced two-party conflict; and lead to the collapse of the Afghanistan government and the Taliban regaining power. It is only by the existence of US troop and NATO troops that make the war in Afghanistan become a somewhat balanced two-party conflict with the involvement of a third party.

The weakness in Afghanistan government is that this government does not present any ideology, and could attract ordinary people from the ideology provided by Taliban. Although the Taliban's belief or ideology is denounced by the US and her allies, the historical fact is that Taliban used their ideology to draw public attention to capture the national power and govern Afghanistan until the US invasion.

The historical lessons drawn here are that a government supported by foreign force could collapse very soon when the leaders in foreign governments are changed because new leaders may have different views and priorities. This aspect has been an important factor for the collapse of many such governments in history. In fact, all the wars conducted in such a landlocked country go against the cost-effectiveness. A clearly important consideration by leaders in foreign governments that support this war in the future.

Even with the possibility of hope to destroy the Taliban and the US and NATO troops could happily go home; Afghanistan still has a large probability to fall into another civil war afterward. In the event that US and NATO troop leave from Afghanistan, a simple fear is because there are so many warlords, who have interest in seizing national power. Perhaps, there remain several options for Afghanistan in the near future.

(1) The US and NATO help to transfer various warlords into various political parties, and then these political parties could then play

political roles in local or national election. If this could be successful, this solution could be possibly to lead to a somewhat similar path of Pakistani political establishment. Meanwhile, the weakness of Afghanistan national army would be an advantage. Afghanistan national army would not play a dominated role in national politics as Pakistani national army does. However, the real problem is if these warlords have political plans that are different one from another. It seems true, each warlord is only interested in seizing power.

(2) The Afghanistan government desperately needs to bring new ideology into this country in order to counterbalance the Taliban's ideology. More assistance is required than merely using the money given by foreign donors. This would be very difficult because not many new ideas appeared attractive in recent years and the western missionary cannot function well in contemporary time. However, if the NATO and US cannot bring in new ideologies; how can the Afghanistan government attract her people away from the Taliban's ideology or other parties in the future?

(3) The international community really needs to think of way to help the Afghanistan people solve their poverty. By introducing a better economic model rather than the production of opium by local people, Afghanistan people can make more money by doing something else rather than sell opium. This is easy to say in plain words but extremely hard to implement. A question raised here is: whether it is possible to integrate the Afghanistan economy into the world? Or to a lesser degree, to somehow alter West Asia's focus from war and conflict in Afghanistan warlords to economic development.

All these solutions may not be possible for this generation, since this generation has lived a considerable time in war. Unfortunately, their mental world is mainly dominated by war and conflict. Perhaps by years of peace for the next generation there could be more interest in economic development.

It is still very interesting as why so many countries have such a great interest in Afghanistan. This country does not impose any danger to the remote world in history and does not show many economic, political or military advantages. All the wars conducted within Afghanistan totally go against the cost-effectiveness. This is a great mystery.

Another totally radical approach to this war, perhaps the only solution for the current situation in Afghanistan as well as for the US government, is to concentrate their efforts on a part of Afghanistan, the part occupied by the current Afghan government. This could produce another divided country in Asia, a part under the US and Afghan government's control and the other under Taliban's loose control.

However, history in Asia, even in Europe, clearly shows that the part under the US control would have an overwhelming economic advantage, which in a long run would beat the part under Taliban's control. Consequently, the better life in the part under the US and Afghan government's control would change the minds of people, who live in the part under Taliban's control. By then, there will be changes because we have seen similar situations between Mainland China and Taiwan, between North Korea and South Korea, even between East Germany and West Germany. This would be the advantage for the US because arguably the US never wins any guerrilla war, which is the very case in Afghanistan, but can easily win any economic war.

4.4. VACUUM IN IRAQ

The current situation in Iraq is an unbalanced two-party conflict, and no party has enough power to win any type of war against the US.

However, the potential hotspot would be after the full withdrawal of US troop from Iraq, because history shows that some countries would fall into chaos after the withdrawal of US troop as in South Vietnam during 70s of the last century [14], i.e., a government supported by US troop would soon collapse after the withdrawal of US troop.

History clearly shows this pattern, that a government supported by various foreign powers and force would soon collapse after the withdrawal of foreign troops, and remaining government is an unstable government.

This would particularly be possible for Iraq, and people could expect to see the conflict between three major ethnic groups. Although this conflict could theoretically be a three-party conflict, it could not be the case because one ethnic group could get a strong support from Iran, and lead to a very unbalanced conflict. No matter if this would occur or not, everyone has the responsibility to prevent conflicts and chaos from occurring. Although, also another possibility is to incorporate two minor ethnic groups to create a new power balance in Iraq after departure of US troop.

On the one hand, there is a possibility to create a relatively balanced three-party conflict in the future Iraqi politics, with the hope to produce a temporary peace for this country. This is with this solution, to create a balance among three ethnic groups in Iraq. This is the view for all the parties inside Iraq at a national level.

At regional level, the withdrawal of US troop from Iraq would undoubtedly create an unbalanced two-party conflict between Iraq and Iran; with the combination of internal ethnic group, this two-party conflict would be very unbalanced and the situation would be unstable.

In general, the influence of Afghanistan on Iraq would be limited because as history shows; a large country generally has influence on small country rather than the opposite; a small country that has influence on a large country. Especially for a country like Afghanistan that is completely landlocked. Although in reference to Africa, this difference shows a small country can influence a big country, but this is not the case in Asia.

The possible solution could be that the US troop continues to stay in Iraq, although currently not many people like this idea. However, if the US troop did not invade Iraq; then it would be meaningless to ask the US troop to come into Iraq, and the two-party conflict between Iraq and Iran would maintain balanced. However, the US troop have occupied Iraq for years; so it would be the US responsibility to maintain the regional power balance and require the US troop to stay in Iraq. Otherwise, either Iraq falls into a chaotic situation or at worst the unbalanced two-party conflict between Iraq and Iran falls into bloodshed. The oil supply to the world would be significantly affected; though this cannot destabilize the world, it could drag the world into another recession.

Chapter 5

CENTRAL ASIA

In general, there is almost no two-party conflict in Central Asia, except for Afghanistan. There are two cases when referring to a no two-party conflict in Central Asia, (i) no third party is really particularly interested in this region, and (ii) there is no direct conflict between any two countries in Central Asia. No endless conflict would provide Central Asia with a real opportunity to make an economic development easier.

However, the Central Asia seems to always be in some phase of economic chronic disease, or in a phase of transition from an old to a new economic model, but have yet to find the best economic model. This gives the impression that these countries may lag behind the world for years. In times when fast economic development occurs in human history the economic chronic disease simply means that the other countries develop fast, while some countries like Central Asia with chronic disease develop slowly. This is similar to a political suicide for the governing parties in power. This is one problem for Central Asia since independence from Russia due to the collapse of Soviet Union.

Asia is very much different from Europe, where many places seem to have adequate roads that are 800 km or less to reach the sea. Existing of excellent roads is unfortunately not the case for Asia and especially, not the case for Central Asia. Although one cannot say that the independence of Central Asia would be economic suicide, the independence leads to a self-imposed shut-off from outside world and a self-introduced economic chronic disease condition.

In this globalized world, the economy in landlocked country is very difficult to develop which makes sense. There is an obvious advantage for the countries that have access to the sea. These countries can be divided into two parts, or even two countries, in terms of developed and undeveloped regions. In these countries, the undeveloped regions are located far away from sea in most cases, while the developed areas in most countries are the place near to the sea. For example, the east and west coasts of US, the coast area in Australia, the coast area in China and India.

Although some of these landlocked countries might be rich in natural resources, unless the landlocked country has the natural resources like crude oil or natural gas; which can easily be transported through pipeline, it is very difficult for landlocked countries to develop. This is simply because the price for transport of natural resources to seaports from landlocked countries is too expensive to make a profit. In fact, the transport of automobiles is already so expensive that most automobile giants build their factories as near as possible to their markets, for example, in the US.

If we lived in the time before any efficient media, the people in these landlocked countries would enjoy their natural surroundings without knowing the development in other places around the world. However, now the people in landlocked countries are impatient with a slow economic development, it is the major factor for the destabilization of the landlocked countries.

However, there is still good opportunity for countries in Central Asia. Now that Russia is not as interested in this region, thus there is no conflict on policy for controlling of Central Asia from Russia; or policy for counter-controlling initiated by Central Asia.

In such a case, there is really no need for Central Asia to be involved in any political disputes and struggles that occur outside Central Asia with international attention. If the countries in Central Asia are not involved, there is a good possibility for quiet development of economy in their remote area.

At this moment, it is important for Central Asia not to introduce any third party into Central Asia, that could perhaps create new two-party conflicts. It is certain that any two-party conflict in Central Asia would eventually have one conflicting party as Russia. Namely, Russia would always be involved in a conflict with any country in Central Asia, because the countries in Central Asia were once included in the Soviet Union. Any two-party conflict with Russia as a party in Central Asia would be an unbalanced two-party conflict, which would lead to a new hotspot in Central Asia.

Currently, any two-party conflict with Russia as an indispensable party is only under surface as a potential conflict. However, the involvement of a third party would make these potential two-party conflicts float on the surface, and would destabilize the Central Asia. The really bitter fact that we must realize is that no third party; such as the US and any other military treaty could function well in this remote Central Asia. The US and NATO are more suitable for a war in oceans or perhaps the European plain but they would be powerless in Central Asia.

Therefore every effort should be made to avoid any further involvement of US military force into Central Asia to generate an unbalanced two-party conflict with the involvement of third party.

One way for fast development in Central Asia is to move towards the direction of sea, which is not to the north but southeast; say, Asia. Asia has a far larger market than ex-USSR for Central Asia. Also Russia is no long hungry for the natural recourses in Central Asia. On the other hand, Asia has far more advanced technologies than the current Russia. Even the countries in Central Asia have already no intention to cooperate with Russia again, nor does Russia.

If the development direction of Central Asia is towards the sea, then Central Asia would have more of a closer economic relationship with China. China now is extremely hungry for various natural recourses, and this would provide important markets for Central Asia. In fact, the northwest of China has a very similar natural condition as most countries in Central Asia. This similarity would provide the basis for development in this area, besides the countries in Central Asia are separate from Soviet Union which once imposed a threat to northwest of China. Also the Islam in countries in Central Asia would not widely spread into China, which would be a concern for the Chinese government. If this new direction of economic development would be successful, it would be a positive economic model for the economic development in Central Asia.

Another economic model for the countries in Central Asia would be the economic model of Switzerland, Austria, and other landlocked European countries. For these countries, the main economic development model is the service, banking, insurance, and high technology. In these specific cases, the vast natural resources in Central Asia seem to be useless for a moment. However, this perhaps could be one of the best economic development models for landlocked countries and could be the economic model for the post-oil era for countries in Central Asia. In fact the countries in Central Asia have such a potential because these countries have a relatively large population that have high education. If the countries in Central Asia pursue the pathway of landlocked European countries, it means that these countries should be absolutely neutral in international and regional affairs. This is a necessary condition for the pursuit of such a development path. This once again requires no involvement of a third party to create any new unbalanced two-party conflicts.

There could be a third economic model for the development of Central Asia, by the development of providing high education services in this region to make money. Several countries surrounding Central Asia have a huge population but need a higher education, especially China for instance. Therefore, by allowing countries in Central Asia into providing higher educational services this could be a way for future economic development.

The fourth possibility for the economic development of Central Asia would be to use the advantage of her time zone that is between Asia and Europe. This means that many traders, even investment banks, would like to sit the countries in Central Asia to trade the securities in Tokyo stock exchange, Chinese stock exchange, Hong Kong stock exchange, as well as other Asian security markets, The advantage is that they would still have time to trade securities in European stock exchanges. This way, the countries in Central Asia would play a similar role as Bahamas islands, where professional traders live and trade the securities in European security markets and then in American markets. In such a case, we would expect to see Las Vegas type cities to be appeared in Central Asia if this could be a possible daydream.

Chapter 6

SOUTH ASIA

The South Asia is far different from other parts of Asia. India is the only dominating country and force in this regional; in clear contrast, there is absolutely no dominating country in East Asia, Central Asia, West Asia, and Southeast Asia. This is very suggestive, to say, it is easy to build a three- or multi-party conflict in East Asia, Central Asia, West Asia, and Southeast Asia, but it is also easy to build an unbalanced two-party conflict or an unbalanced two-party conflict with the involvement of a regional third party; by clear contrast, it is not easy to build any balanced-conflict in South Asia.

Therefore, India does play an extremely important role in stability and economic development in South Asia on the one hand. However, it would be reasonable to say that the really unstable factor in South Asia would be the rise of India with her ambition to dominate the regional affairs in South Asia.

This is by no means to deny the great positive and constructive role that India has played or will play. In fact, India should be a permanent member in UN Security Council with her unique contribution to the world, and all Asian countries should support this initiative.

The problem that is plausible for India, which appears more regional, on the world stage as a new power, with new unfamiliar position, may consequently abuse her power as an Indian version of Monroe doctrine in the affairs in South Asia. First of all, this implies that Indian should develop a well-considered plan before exercising her power in South Asia. Moreover, this also implies that either a regional power or a world power needs time to learn how to correctly and efficiently use her regional or world entitlement [2]. There would be a learning curve for any emerging powers that include China.

Perhaps, the historical lessons for any new emerging power would be how Germany tried to exercise her entitlement as a new emerged world power during World Wars I and II, and how Japan tried to exercise her entitlement as a new emerged regional power during World War II.

Perhaps, the best way to prevent the abuse of entitlement by a new emerging regional power or a new emerging world power would limit her role in regional affairs but encourage her to play her role in international affairs; which, generally is beyond the military force of new emerging power.

Therefore, it would be the duty of other Asian countries to encourage India to be more and more involved in international affairs, but discourage India's involvement in regional conflicts. The aim here is to avoid an unbalanced two-party conflict in South Asia or an unbalanced two-party conflict with the involvement of India.

Similarly and ironically, there would be a learning curve for any declining powers on how to adequately use their new positions without speeding up their decline.

6.1. PROBLEMS AND SOLUTIONS

6.1.1. India-Pakistan Conflict

A full-scale war between India and Pakistan is very unlikely to occur, may even be impossible to occur, because both countries can retaliate with nuclear weapons.. Therefore, this creates a somewhat balanced two-party conflict in sense of the possibility of a nuclear retaliation. For a balanced two-party conflict, the best way to maintain this balance is to avoid the third party involvement. Currently the only effective third party is the US government, which in the past consistently supported Pakistan. Now the US government has changed her mind to some degree due to the difficulty in war against

Taliban, and other issues. This leads the US government to increase her interest in India. This new alliance would consequently create an unbalanced two-party conflict between India and Pakistan, because as history has shown India is more likely to be involved in a war if a third party stands with her, for example, India's involvement in Sino-Indian war in 1962, independence of Bangladesh, and civil war in Sri Lanka.

A possible way that is to reduce the engagement of the US in India would be to prevent the US government from changing her mind to give up on Pakistan. The involvement of Russia with India has potential since both countries have a better relationship. However, if Russia would become too interested in India, the US would be more likely to support Pakistan, and would result in a balanced two-party conflict with the involvement of a third party. In such a case, one would consider the return to a similar situation of during the Cold War, when the US and Soviet Union balanced each other in many ways in many countries.

However, it appears to have no obvious solution to the balanced two-party conflict between India and Pakistan. Even if the conflict in Kashmir could have eventually been solved; India and Pakistan would find another point to confront each other on. Perhaps, if people leave this endless two-party conflict balanced is arguably the best solution because it creates a permanent peace in this region.

6.1.2. Sri Lanka Civil War

The recent defeat of the Tamil Tigers is clear evidence, because it clearly shows how an unbalanced two-party conflict cannot continue for a long time; where in Sri Lanka's past, its region was partially balanced by India as a third party. Meanwhile, the weak party in an unbalanced two-party conflict has the ability to use various means against the strong party, like for instance suicide bombings.

In reality, this conflict is similar to the independent movement in North Ireland and Basque regions. History in these two regions does not provide any clear solution, either military or peaceful, even in those very democratic countries.

Hopefully, with the end of this dreadful civil war, economic development in war-troubled zone could lead to reconciliation. A peaceful role that only India can play is clear, because other countries are not only far away from this bloody conflict but also lack regional interests. Thus, the best solution realistically for Sri Lanka is to enter the economic cluster in South Asia.

6.1.3. Sino-Indian Conflict

The unsettled border dispute would always be a potential hotspot for China and India. When both countries have no other major concerns, their focus someday will once again spontaneously converge upon this border issue. Once that happens, then there is the possibility of a deterioration in the relationship between India and China, as history has proven.

In the Asian stage, it seems that China and India have always been rivals; despite of the fact that both countries have different cultures, traditions, interests, approaches, social systems, and so forth. Moreover, these two countries are in effect separated by Himalayas Mountains.

In fact, the western media plays an important, but unconstructive role in promotion for a hypothetical competition between China and India. The western media never compares China with Japan nor compares India with Japan. It is fantasy that neither China nor India would like to compare herself with Japan, but rather compare the development between China and India. Under the comparisons initiated by western media, China and India always are rivals to each other. Moreover, the western media labels the economic development in China and India with different social mechanisms and different ideologies. Thus the economic development in both countries becomes a competition between socialism and capitalism, as it was labeled between US and Soviet Union in the last century. This is a sad aspect of current media [15].

In fact, the Chinese have never entered the Indian Ocean in any significant way, while the Indians has never had any dispute related to China. China and

India have had no direct conflicts besides their border dispute. Also both countries have less common interests;, the Indians are more interested in the UK while the Chinese are more interested in the US. The economic development in China focuses more on industry while the economic development in India focuses more on service. There is really no need to create a so-called competition between China and India.

Under this poisonous comparison, the tension between China and India would finally increase. This in fact would be harmful for India, because India would have to open another balanced two-party conflict plus currently balance a two-party conflict with Pakistan. Also the unbalanced two-party conflict, although finished now in Sri Lanka. These three potential hostile two-party conflicts related to India would be new, if not the first case in Indian history.

On the other hand, this potential conflict between China and India demonstrates how much old the thought is influenced by western media. This is not a constructive and peaceful aspect and the kind of thought inherited from the Cold War.

Therefore, it is for India's best interest not to open a third two-party conflict with China, because China currently is not involved in any two-party conflict besides the conflict with Taiwan.

6.1.4. Solution

The solution appears simple; every effort should be made to keep the US government away from fully supporting India, since it would destabilize South Asia. In fact, the current trend suggests that the US government is moving away from supporting of Pakistan and has more interest in India. The US government is mainly not happy with the progress that Pakistan has done to fight Taliban. However, no matter how little the progress is, Pakistan is still doing something. India certainly cannot be involved in any direct conflict with Taliban.

Without US support in Pakistan, the economy would become worse and could enter into a chaotic and unstable situation with an unfavorable outcome of more militant group influence.

Meanwhile, a better perspective for a stable Pakistan would be good for India, since India cannot receive any significant gain or benefit from potential chaos in Pakistan; just as South Korea cannot profit from the collapse of North Korea.

No one denies the fact that India is a regional power whose influence can lead to many unbalanced two-party conflicts in South Asia. In order to maintain the peace in South Asia, it is therefore the responsibility of a world power, like the US; to balance all these unbalanced two-party conflicts by direct engagement with weaker party.

The problem between China and India is yet to settle and a reasonable approach to reducing this tension between China and India is to open their common border. The hope in this case would be to promote more economic development in these disputed border regions.

6.2. FAVORABLE AND UNFAVORABLE POINTS

The greatest favorable point and best advantage for India is its unique position in the Indian Ocean, where there is no other regional power to challenge her; and, no world power that can pour so much money to compete with India. Therefore, it is very possible for India to focus her efforts for economic development along Indian Ocean Rim, which would provide excellent opportunity that could be comparable to the opportunities provided along Pacific Rim. This means that India might be more likely to be involved in Africa, where the US is afraid to be involved but gives India the opportunity..

The only unfavorable point is that India might not need to militarily dominate Indian Ocean, simply because it is not necessary. However, the Indian military establishment might not be happy for the limited role of only having influence in Indian Ocean.

Chapter 7

SOUTHEAST ASIA

The truth in Southeast Asia is that it has fewer and less extensive conflicts and hotspots than any other regions in Asia. The limited number of random conflicts is not on national levels at all, and therefore there is no balanced or unbalanced two-party conflict between two countries. The implication for this region is that we do no need to use either balanced or unbalanced two-party conflict to analyze this region.

This region has already had a long and quite successful ASEAN; yet, this ASEAN does not include any economic giants as in Asia. Although ASEAN was a good frame or platform for the development as a model in the past, its speed efficiency is certainly disappointing considering that ASEAN already has a 50-plus-year history.

Perhaps, it is ASEAN itself that feels the slow development unbearable and thus, proposes a much closer economic relationship with East Asia. This is a wise decision and the easiest way to create a free trade zone either within the frame of ASEAN, or between ASEAN and East Asia. Although some politicians advocate a single currency as a trial in ASEAN; it is very unlikely that the ASEAN would adopt any single currency, especially when China would be involved in ASEAN. Most countries in ASEAN would be happy to make money from China, but are afraid of a strong Chinese influence on their society. This region has already a strong influence by the prevalence of either the spoken Chinese language or its Chinese basic culture.

In realty, this region can be regarded as partly or completely Americanized. Therefore any initiative would be difficult to implement without the approval from the US, which seems not to be very interested in a single currency system for ASEAN. On the other hand, this region has the smallest ambition either in political or international affairs, inherited from the Chinese tradition [2]. The ASEAN has a very quiet region either in the Asian stage or international stage. Thus the so-called single currency in ASEAN would have very small impact.

Honestly, South Asia as China is one of places where their people are open to any measures that would make their lives better.

The involvement of countries from East Asia would be vital for further economic development of ASEAN, since the way for economic development within ASEAN seems to be exhausted.

Perhaps the best place to begin is with China as having a closer economic relationship between ASEAN and East Asia, and so-called Indochina.

The problem with so-called French Indochina is her unstable economic development, and how vulnerable it is to any turbulence in the world economy. This means that most small countries without natural resources are very vulnerable to any economic slowdown in the world as a result of globalization. However, small countries should be involved in globalization to pursue their own economic development. The key point here is, how could small countries design an approach of development that is less sensitive to an economic turmoil in the world?

So the problem for this Indochina region would be how to overcome their vulnerability? A reasonable solution would be a shared risk. One way to share this risk is a shared risk among countries that would have a relatively small economic power. The gain for this approach is that the economy could be independent, but the loss is that these countries with small economic power might not be able to resist against a relatively severe economic slowdown.

Another way for this shared risk among these countries is to have a relatively large economic power. The fear for this kind of approach is obvious, because a country with small economic power is afraid for her identity or is afraid that her economy would be controlled by a large economic power.

However, the challenge and opportunity for this region is that the economic model is directed toward export. So why do they not make money from East Asia?

For the Indochina region, the best way is to integrate into Chinese economic cluster with a multi-currency system, as with Vietnam, Laos, and Cambodia. These three countries have a good relationship with China in history, and generally follow the Chinese culture closely.

In essence, there is little difference in the living habits between the people in south of China and the people in Vietnam, Laos, and Cambodia. In addition, the thinking patterns are very similar to people living in these regions and people living in China. Besides, the political systems in effect are quite similar for Vietnam, Laos, and China with the exception of Cambodia. These aspects are important for a close economic relationship with Vietnam, Laos, and Cambodia, especially, since Vietnam would have a massive market for rice, shoes, and receive the massive investment from Chinese.

However, the great difference in language among these four countries would efficiently prevent massive immigrants.

There seem to be no losers for this kind of economic cluster, simply because the weather in Vietnam, Laos, and Cambodia is too hot for the Chinese to work there. Vietnam, Laos, and Cambodia could enjoy the tax advantage collected from Chinese merchants, who are generally the first group of people to go abroad when a border opens. China would gain through this exporting her goods and reduce the unemployment pressure.

Another big problem in South Asia would be Burma, whose economy is hopeless and her political system comes in the second as the most corrupted in the world [16]. There is no way to get out from this difficulty through any economic reform under this regime. Fortunately, this country does not impose any danger to the outside world, or has no ability to endanger outside world. Thus, the people around the world could let her go her own way.. Perhaps there are some ways for political reforms, but do not seem to be attractive. The hope would be for the distant future, when the surrounding countries are far richer than Burma. The unhappy young military officers could initiate another coup d'etat, and might pave the way for complete change in Burma. Arguably this would be a great opportunity for the international community to draw Burma back into the Asian family as well as international family.

Chapter 8

ASIAN UNION INITIATIVE

All the proposed solutions to the various conflicts in Asia are related to actions of not only stopping these conflicts, but also encouraging economic development.

Therefore, any Asian Union initiative should have two specific aims that are extremely important for the Asian people, (i) hope to stop the endless conflicts in Asia, and (ii) hope to promote the economic development in Asia.

On an Asian level, it seems that the conditions are ready for the creation of an Asian Union in terms of economy. Previous discussions seemed impossible and extremely poor in terms of cost-effectiveness for an Asian Union when dealing with the aspects of political, religious, or military union.

Although, the very short-term experience from the European Union could suggest that a single currency system would be the essence for any economic union. The Asian Union seems dauntingly complex. History shows that many historical attempts to create a single currency eventually failed [17]. Moreover, the single currency policy in European Union apparently does not bring many advocated advantages to its economy, and does not make European Union immune to a worldwide economic slowdown.

Although many scholars would suggest that the best way to create an economic Asian Union would be the creation of a single currency, within all Asian countries, it seems to be impossible and unrealistic for Asia. The idea of one central bank to set an interest rate for all Asian countries would be a hard sell. Each Asian country has her own development approach, with her own problems concerning development and are in different stages of development. Moreover, many Asian governments would consider their currency as the sovereignty and would be afraid of any application of a single currency.

Also, we could say that the single currency does not work well within European Union because the economic situation is very different between and among countries, as for example between Germany and Spain. A country might need to increase her interest rate to beat inflation, while another country might need to decrease her interest rate to promote her export and stimulate her economy. Still, the single currency is very costly, since each country needs to adopt this new system, even more costly in considering the population size in Asia.

It is also impossible to build several regional central banks in Tokyo, Shanghai, Singapore, Hong Kong, Jerusalem, Bombay, Teheran. For instance, to set interest rates for each regionally economic cluster and oversee what is happening in each country is inconceivable. Asian countries are so different, and there is doubt that Pakistani government could allow a bank in Bombay to decide her interest rate.

Therefore, a more workable and realistic solution would be at first to create several economic clusters in Asia. The currencies in the same clusters could be used in all countries in the same economic cluster. This means that each country would accept different currencies from the countries in the same cluster and the settlement would be done when dealing with any particular currency in the same economic cluster.

This way, to promote the economic development at regional Asian level, and Asia could become more stable. The multi-currency system in fact would be better than a single currency system in Asia, because it reduces the worry that a big country could control a small country in Asia. The multi-currency system would have the least impact on political system in each individual country. On the other hand, the multi-currency system could promote the exchange of people, facilitate the trade and improve life-style in Asia. Again, this way, Asian people could know and understand each other more, and perhaps better; thus reduce the chance of conflict and make Asia and the world more peaceful.

In fact, the decisive force to create several economic clusters with a multi-currency system in Asia is in the hands of governing parties, but not in the hands of Asian people. There are a few countries in Asia that are not democratic countries, and thus these Asian people have little chance to participate in any decision-making processes as the Americans and Europeans do. As a result, the advantage for a governing party to apply an idea to her own country is if the application could benefit to this very governing party at first. After meeting this strict condition, then a governing party would consider if the application could be a benefit to the people governed. Therefore any new mechanisms, should not threaten a governing party and would have a good chance to be introduced into Asia and survive.

One the other hand, this also creates an opportunity to introduce any new mechanisms into Asia easily because there is no referendum needed in any Asian country. The only way is to convince the governing party. and influence the internal politics.

In short, a way out of endless conflicts in Asia would arguably be by various political systems at a national level, but with emphasis on the integration of economics at an Asian level. The creation of an Asian Union could be an important solution to various problems facing the Asian countries.

8.1. PROBLEM

Although the proposed Asian Union initiative is an economic union, the focus would be concentrated on solving regional conflicts followed with economic development; or at least finding a solution to conflicts and economic development should be weighted equally.

From a viewpoint of international politics, the proposed Asian Union would not function. Even if established by Asia, it would not get the support from the US government and European Union, or even the UN, to a large extent, any Asian Union would not function well without the understanding, endorsements and support from international communities. Therefore, every effort should be made to get the understanding and support from international communities. At this moment, the most likely supporters could come from the European Union and Africa, then Australasia; and finally the US government.

However, the proposed solution would impose a big problem for the Asian countries because Asia has yet to become developed enough on the world stage; as evidenced in the European Union or the United States of America with homogenous economic systems and similar living standards.

In Asia for example, the living standard varies greatly and is different from country to country; and the economic mechanisms are very different from country to country. In addition, Asian countries generally have no easy-access-borders, and have very different languages, very different cultures, very different traditions, etc.

On the positive side, these differences would prevent large-scale economic immigrations between countries, and the fear of the richer Asian countries. On the negative side, these differences would also prevent free trade between countries, and would prevent benefits to both rich or poor Asian countries alike.

For economic development it could be possible to form several economic clusters in Asia, although there are already several such cluster-type inter-country organizations such as ASEAN. However, these organizations have yet to reach the level of multi-currency system, free trade, free movement of people, and open their borders completely.

Even over the next five or ten decades, it would be impossible for Asian countries to form a Union under the same constitution, since the regimes are so different. A possible step would be economic clusters throughout Asia. These clusters could be totally different from the current version of inter-country organizations or could be a further development from current version; for example, the ASEAN could be a starting point.

Thus, the potential problem for Asian Union in terms of economic cluster would be: how to form these clusters? The hope here is to solve the regional conflicts through economic clusters.

8.2. SOLUTION

Reasonably and reliably, the Asian Union would include several economic clusters rather than a single economic cluster as the European Union. Each economic cluster would be in some form of current trade blocs; for examples, Asia-Pacific Economic Cooperation, Asia-Europe Economic Meeting, Association of Southeast Asian Nations, Gulf Cooperation Council, Closer Economic Partnership Arrangement, Commonwealth of Independent States, South Asian Association for Regional Cooperation, etc. Based on these blocs, the free trade zone, multi-currency system, free movement of people and open borders could be considered possible and could be implemented. There are several possible ways to create these economic clusters.

8.2.1. Economic Cluster Based on Political System

Several economic clusters could be created based on a political system, and is quite suitable for some countries that have no desire to see any Asian countries with different political systems from theirs. In such a case, Burma however, would be excluded from most Asian countries because her political system is quite different from other Asian countries, and has no desire to meet any countries with a different political system. Along this line, China, North Korea, Vietnam, and Laos would be considered as the same political system to build a close economic cluster.

The advantage for this type of cluster would be that the same or similar economic model and mechanism are running for the entire economic cluster with little local difference, and would result in little resistance at a national or provincial level. Thus, the economic negotiations could be simple and easy, although the most important point would be to avoid possible influence on their own political establishments.

8.2.2. Economic Cluster Based on Language

Several economic clusters could be created based on the same or similar language system. This way, such economic clusters would include countries in West Asia, where the Arabic language is the official language or is the popular language. Nevertheless, this would be a huge advantage for free movement of people within this economic cluster in question. The biggest disadvantage would be that the same language would make it easier for the transmission of ideas, and this might not be a welcomed outcome in certain countries.

8.2.3. Economic Cluster Based on GDP

The rich Asian countries would certainly not be happy with the concept that their economic cluster would include the poor Asian countries, and this concept could hurt their pride. This is understandable, for example Hong Kong is unlikely to have great interest to work with very poor countries. Hence, several economic clusters could be composed of similar GDP Asian countries; which, in fact, is the current model to distinguish the countries that adopted Euro from the countries that will adopt Euro in the future. The great advantage nevertheless is to prevent the flood of economic immigrants from the poor Asian countries, and the disadvantage of rich countries would be that they lack the people who would like to take a low salary to do simply physical work.

8.2.4. Economic Cluster Based on Religion

This solution could also be very attractive and could function well in some parts of Asia, although the really religious people might have less interests in economic developments than politicians do. However, ordinary people might have a natural intention to trust the people with the same religion, and the trades would then be much easier. This type of economic cluster could easily lead to the free trade zone and free movement of people, while both are important steps for economic development.

8.2.5. Economic Cluster Based on Geographic Location

We could also see the creation of economic clusters according to the traditionally geographic locations in Asia, and expect to see economic clusters in East Asia, South Asia, West Asia, Central Asia, and Southeast Asia, respectively. This could be a solution associated with initiatives to solve the endless conflicts and to cool down the hotspots in each region. Perhaps this is a better way to bring peace in each region.

8.2.6. Economic Complimentary Cluster

All these approaches to create economic clusters mentioned here suffer the problem that the economy in any given cluster might not be complimentary, especially when an economic cluster is small. Therefore, the creation of an economic cluster based on an economic feature would be complementary could combine the countries, and where the economy has a different focus. That is, a country with stronger agriculture but weaker industry would integrate with a country with weaker agriculture but stronger industry. Still the country with stronger service industry would integrate with the country with weaker service industry.

8.3. FAVORABLE AND UNFAVORABLE POINTS

Several economic clusters possessing various economic mechanisms, the unnecessary but painful and sorrowful economic competition between Asian countries could be minimized if not completely avoided. For the imbalance in economy, the free trade, free movement of people and multi-currency system would be a solution.

Certainly many countries would not be happy with the idea that their economy could be incorporated with the economy of their conflicting party. For example, Pakistan would certainly not be happy with the possibility as an incorporation of her economy with Indian economy. However, this could be overcome through the adoption of several currencies used in another yet different Asian economic cluster. That is, a country could join different Asian economic clusters, and accept different Asian currencies as legitimate currencies.

This way, each Asian country would enjoy the economic benefit from the economic development and share the risk raised within the given economic cluster or from outside of her economic cluster. Even enjoy the economic benefit and share the risk among several economic clusters, if the country would adopt several currencies.

Of course, this would create a huge amount of research in this field with regard to how the economy in each country would behave if the country would have several legitimate currencies. However, another issue that is of less worry, would be that it would be very hard to manipulate and control the economy in other Asian countries using the tool of single currency. This would be huge advantage for Asian countries, where there always is be a fear of loss their sovereignty.

The Asian economic cluster would have learnt the expensive lesson from the European Union in adopting the single currency, which required all the members to switch to the Euro as the single currency overnight. The best way for Asian economic clusters would be to allow different Asian currencies circulating simultaneously in certain countries.

The simultaneous circulation of several currencies in a certain country would stabilize her economy not only because all the risks would be shared by countries holding any of these several currencies, but also the overthrowing of old government by means of either revolution or coup d'etat would not mean to change the currency since this currency is already circulating in different countries. The new government should honor her currency. This would greatly reduce the possibility of the collapse in their economy, and promote the political stability in Asian countries.

By this mechanism where several Asian currencies simultaneously circulate in a given country, the people might favor a certain currency at the initial phase. The long-term trend is unlikely to abandon some currencies but to favor one currency, because it is hard to imagine a currency could easily dominate an economic cluster that is built based on the similarity of a political, or language, or GDP, or religion, or geographic location, or economic complimentary feature.

The free movement of people would bring the boom of tourism in Asia. Asia has the most diversity in culture, development, and religion. Thus, the Asian Union would bring the best chance for the tourism industry and related service in Asia and create millions of jobs in related services. Besides, the Asian people would know far better about Asia herself, and understand the difference in culture and religion. This is the way to avoid the conflict. This would require minimizing the visa application process and even visa-free for a certain economic cluster plus the multi-currency system applied in the given economic cluster. Although this visa-free process would appear dangerous for some countries, the real fact would not be so dreadful because the big difference in languages, cultures and job-hunting at an Asian level would discourage the possible immigration.

The unfavorable point would perhaps be the initial pains for the countries undergoing such an economic cluster, and would be a common phenomenon for any type of reform. However, the job of politicians should be their leadership to make the economic development with the fewest pains as possible.

This way, Asia will have the potential to possess the most active economy in the world, and for the future. Asia would have the potential to possess the largest markets with respect to size of population and territory, and play a peaceful and constructive role in the world. We might say here, that this process would be the regionalization that corresponds to globalization. Asian people can do a regionalization inside Asia according to the principle of globalization by the integration of our economy.

Chapter 9

RUSSIA AND TURKEY
BACK TO ASIAN FAMILY

No one could doubt the fact that there would be more chances for economic development in Asia than in Europe. Asia now has a fast economic development and a market with a huge population size; therefore it could be reasonable for Turkey and Russia to pay more attention to integrate their economy into one of the Asian clusters.

Historically, Turkey has been focused on Europe since the time of the Trojan war [18], then Byzantine Empire [19], and Ottoman Empire [20]. However, this tradition is not functioning well due to the setback that Turkey has desperately been trying for years to enter the European Union. And, it is still highly unlikely for Turkey to enter the European Union. The endless efforts to gain entry into the European Union are a bitter disappointment for the Turkish people. Not to mention the numerous demands and requests from European Union to meet certain conditions, which might be unreachable.

Now with no other choice at hand, the Turkish people could consider to move their focus away from Europe, possibly consider Asia, especially West Asia, although the endless conflict with Kurd in the Iraqi region has already drawn some attention from Turkish people to the West Asia.

Therefore, there would be a big probability to incorporate Turkey into Asian Union. The return of Turkey into the Asian family would balance the influence of Iran and create a stable and peaceful prospective in West Asia.

The improvement for relationship between Turkey and Iran would be crucial to reduce the tension in Middle East. To draw Iran back into the international community and slowdown the nuclear program in Iran, and reduce Iranian hostile attitude to Israel is a promising step.

Moreover, Turkey, as an example of a Muslim country that is rapidly transformed into a liberal democratic country; that would lead to the construction of a democratic elected bloc of countries in Middle East, as well as West Asia could greatly reduce the tension in this region.

There is the possibility that a large amount of oil and gas passing from Iran through Turkey to Europe could reduce the tension in Persian Gulf and Strait of Hormuz, and further reduce the danger of war in this region. The new pipeline between Turkey and Iran would create a massive amount of jobs, and thus would reduce the unemployment rate in Iran. The Turkish government would take less risk to divert the attention of Iranians from the conflict.

On the other hand, there are few Muslim countries in Europe, but plenty of Muslim countries in the West Asia. Therefore Turkish people would feel more comfortable in West Asia, and Turkey could serve as the best example for development and democracy.

For Turkey, Asia doubtlessly provides an important opportunity for her development. This means that Turkey would improve her relationship with Iran, Syria, and Iraq.

In general, Turkey would gain from her economic integration with Asian economy. Especially when considering the West Asia economic cluster, because this would be a deal for peace instead of war, since Turkish history shows that Turkey is very likely to be involved in wars with European countries rather than with Asian countries.

At this moment it is hard to see any disadvantages for a Turkish return to Asian family, because the US government would be happy to have Turkey to deal with Iran rather than the US herself does. the US would be happy to have a member of NATO to penetrate into West Asia, be satisfied not to endorse

Turkey to enter European Union, etc. European Union would be happy to have fewer disputes with Turkey concerning its potential membership.

The problem for Russia would be endless frictions with European countries and NATO, as they encroach on Russian's border everyday. Now the question is whether these endless frictions can create a balanced two-party conflict to maintain the stability in Europe? The answer seems to be yes, because the countries surrounding Russia are too powerless and small to make any really serious challenge against Russia. Moreover, these countries that joined the NATO have no real intention to challenge Russia, but would like to have a better and stable life under the guarantee of a NATO treaty.

This simply means that Russia would still have a peaceful time in this balanced two-party conflict with NATO for a long time. European history shows that the European politics were largely decided by European powers rather than the small countries surrounding Russia. If this hypothetical case were true, then Russia would focus her efforts on economic development and might suggest that Russian's focus on Europe could move toward Asia step-by-step.

The problem would again be if the Russian government would gain from such a strategic transformation to change focus from Europe to Asia. The answer again is positive, because (i) politically the Russian government would have far fewer conflicts with Asian countries when she develops her Asian part, while there would be always unhappiness when Russia develops towards the west. (ii) Culturally, Russia is truly a country mixed with Asian and European cultures, and this gives a great advantage for Russia to integrate into any Asian economic clusters. Russian people would not feel as strange toward the Asian culture. The incorporation of Russian economy with Asian economy would benefit both Russia and Asian countries. (iii) Nevertheless, the Asian market would need more oil, gas, and other raw materials from Russia than European market do.

However, if these three points are not convincing enough, the most convincing point for Russia to change her focus from Europe to Asia would be the global warming. Now it seems to be certain that humans cannot efficiently and effectively reverse the global warming within one or two generations. In such a case, the Siberia is frequently regarded as Sahara; would become a place more suited for economic development in terms of either agriculture or industry. The economic development in Siberia would draw more attention from investors all over the world, because this could be the last place in this planet to be invested. For the economic development in Siberia, not only money is needed, but people also are needed. The density of population in Siberia, even Russia herself, could not support such a large-scale economic development in Siberia.

The only place in the world that could provide such a sizable working force would be Asia, to less extent, Africa. The Asian people would be more interested in economic development in Siberia then Europeans or Americans would be. This could lead to the open borders between Russia and China, and between Russia and North Korea; to allow Chinese and Korean to work in Siberia, and a multi-currency system to be implemented among Russia, North Korea, China, even Japan. This could lead to a lasting peace in East Asia, and further reduce the tension led by the nuclear program in North Korea.

Therefore, arguably the global warming would be helpful to Russia and lead to her government to change focus from Europe to Asia. This could be the most basic reason as to why Russia should come back to Asian family.

The territorial dispute between Russia and Japan could draw less attention with the economic development in Siberia, because the investment opportunities would postpone the desire to solve this problem in near future. Politics is governed by money.

In general, Russia and Turkey would bring very important European ideas and working methods to Asia. This would be extremely good for the development in Asia, because traditionally Asia was weaker than Europe and the European methods could change the philosophy in Asia to some degree and make Asia more modernized.

Chapter 10

US ROLE IN CHANGING WORLD

Realistically, any union or international organization would not be successful without the endorsement from the US government. The fate of Non-Aligned Movement would serve as an example, that dreamed to form an international organization without any involvement of major world power [21]; but has its difficulty to do anything efficiently and effectively.

Therefore the first job for the proposed Asian Union initiative would be to get the support from the US government. This would be the great trust that Asian people would put on the US government in changing the world.

This great trust means that the US government would have to change her policy on many aspects; in order to restore her currently less-respected position to a more-respected position in the world. This is because (i) the current US economic power is far smaller than after World War II, (ii) the freedom and democracy promoted by the US have decreased for more than a half a century,and is disgraced day by day, and (iii) the US life style becomes less and less attractive due to the economic development in other parts of the world.

The differences between the time after World War II and the present are the huge challenges facing the US policy makers, who desperately need to plan a new way or several new ways to maintain her position in the world.

Unfortunately, existing old school thought inherited from the Cold War is still prevalent. For instance, the thought held before September 11 by the Bush administration was still to confront Russia, even though Russia was no longer a world power. The economic cost in the war on terror suggests that the US economy cannot bear the big burden due, by wars designed by old school thought [22]. The US foreign policy was often to concentrate on how the US could be involved in a conflict as quickly and fast as possible, but not able to fully consider how the US could be disengaged from a conflict as honorable scenario as possible after initial involvement.

This means that each country needs to consider a way out from a troubled involvement before really engaging in it. History already repeatedly shows how a powerful country that hastily gets involved in a conflict or hastily initiates a conflict, tends to create disaster.

Through strong world entitlement, the US government should at first consider ways to avoid involvement in any two-party conflict before committing to anything. In the past, the US withdrew from her involvements and frequently left a new unbalanced two-party conflict and caused great pains for both the US and conflicting parties.

The focus of the US government should move away from current policy and mainly base US interests on leading the unbalanced two-party conflict around the world. By the role to maintain the balanced two-party conflicts around the world, the US can improve their image abroad immensely.

This means that the US government should try to balance the unbalanced two-party conflicts around the world rather than to unbalance the balanced two-party conflict around the world, because currently the US is the only country in the world to have such an ability to make a two-party conflict either balanced or unbalanced.

Since World War II, many young men and young women have studied in the US and have been influenced by US thoughts around the world. These thoughts and ideas promote prosperity around the world. By clear contrast, fewer Americans have studied outside the US and therefore fewer, if any thoughts back to the US.

This is to say that people around the world know and understand the US. Universally, other people are able to understand US concepts, their thoughts, the life style, traditions, culture, movies, songs, holidays, etc. possibly, perhaps far better than the people in the US do. The direct consequence is that the people in the US are ignorant of the world. How can the US government play a fair and just role under such circumstance? How can the US intelligence agencies function well and give correct advice to the US government?

This means that the American people really need to go abroad, and not only for tourism; but also more importantly, to sit patiently and study every thing seriously in foreign countries. This way, the US government could get really valuable information to exercise her role for changing the world. The half-life of a decaying US economy with reference to her contribution to the world economy suggests that in another half a century the US economy would still hold the leading position in the world [2]. This gives the US power to exercise her world entitlement on the world stage.

This way, not only the United States of America could continue to contribute to the world peace and prosperity, but also the United States of Asia would continue to contribute to the world peace and prosperity.

REFERENCES

[1]   Wu, G., and Yan, S. (2008). *Lecture Notes on Computational Mutation*. New York: Nova Science Publishers.

[2]   Wu, G. (2009). China: *Has the Last Opportunity Passed By?!* New York: Nova Science Publishers.

[3]   http://en.wikipedia.org/wiki/Asian_Century.

[4]   Aesop. (2004). *Aesop's Fables*. Project Gutenberg, eBook # 11339.

[5]   Tan, S. 2003. The 'United States of Asia.' A possibility today? Asia Europe J 1: 159-161.

[6]   http://en.wikipedia.org/wiki/Israel-Egypt_peace_agreement.

[7]   http://en.wikipedia.org/wiki/Three_Kingdom_era

[8]   http://www.amazon.com/Strategy-Conflict-Thomas-C-Schelling/product-reviews/0674840305/ref=cm_cr_dp_hist_4?ie=UTF8&showViewpoints =0&filterBy=addFourStar

[9]   http://en.wikipedia.org/wiki/Russo-Japanese_War

[10] http://en.wikipedia.org/wiki/Korean_War#Invasion_of_South_Korea

[11] http://en.wikipedia.org/wiki/Israel-Jordan_Treaty_of_Peace

[12] http://en.wikipedia.org/wiki/Military_strategy

[13] http://en.wikipedia.org/wiki/Afghanistan

[14] http://en.wikipedia.org/wiki/South_Vietnam

[15] Davies N. *Flat Earth News: An Award-Winning Reporter Exposes Falsehood, Distortion and Propaganda in the Global Media*. London: Random House, 2009.

[16] http://en.wikipedia.org/wiki/Corruption_Perceptions_Index

[17] http://en.wikipedia.org/wiki/Single_currency

[18] http://en.wikipedia.org/wiki/Troy_War

[19] http://en.wikipedia.org/wiki/Eastern_Roman_Empire

[20] http://en.wikipedia.org/wiki/Ottoman_Empire

[21] http://en.wikipedia.org/wiki/Nonalignment

[22] Barnett, T.P.M. (2009). *Great Powers: America and the World After Bush*. New York: Putnam Adult.

INDEX